1/7/11

DEMCO 38-296

Discount Business Strategy

Discount Business Strategy

How the New Market Leaders are Redefining Business Strategy

Michael Moesgaard Andersen and Flemming Poulfelt

John Wiley & Sons, Ltd

Other Wiley Editorial Offices

John Wiley & Sons Inc., 111 River Street, Hoboken, NJ 07030, USA

Jossey-Bass, 989 Market Street, San Francisco, CA 94103-1741, USA

Wiley-VCH Verlag GmbH, Boschstr. 12, D-69469 Weinheim, Germany

John Wiley & Sons Australia Ltd, 42 McDougall Street, Milton, Queensland 4064, Australia

John Wiley & Sons (Asia) Pte Ltd, 2 Clementi Loop #02-01, Jin Xing Distripark, Singapore 129809

John Wiley & Sons Canada Ltd, 22 Worcester Road, Etobicoke, Ontario, Canada M9W 1L1

Wiley also publishes its books in a variety of electronic formats. Some content that appears in
print may not be available in electronic books.

Library of Congress Cataloging in Publication Data

Andersen, Michael Moesgaard.
    Discount business strategy : how the new market leaders are redefining business
    strategy / Michael Moesgaard Andersen & Flemming Poulfelt.
       p.   cm.
    Includes bibliographical references and index.
    ISBN-13: 978-0-470-03353-1 (cloth : alk. paper)
    ISBN-10: 0-470-03353-3 (cloth : alk. paper)
    1. Organizational effectiveness.   2. Industrial efficiency.   3. Industrial management—
    Case studies.   4. Discount houses (Retail trade)   I. Poulfelt, Flemming.   II. Title.
    HD58.9.A534 2006
    658.4′012—dc22   2006018007

British Library Cataloguing in Publication Data

A catalogue record for this book is available from the British Library

ISBN-13 978-0-470-03353-1 (HB)
ISBN-10 0-470-03353-3 (HB)

Typeset in 11/16pt Trump Medieval by Integra Software Services Pvt. Ltd, Pondicherry, India
Printed and bound in Great Britain by TJ International Ltd, Padstow, Cornwall, UK
This book is printed on acid-free paper responsibly manufactured from sustainable forestry
in which at least two trees are planted for each one used for paper production.

Contents

Foreword

SOME YEARS AGO WE WERE BOTH SITTING AT BOARD MEETINGS, having the usual discussions covering questions like: How do we create sustainable advantages? Can we mitigate competition? What is our trade off between producing better products and achieving lower prices? Do we have competitive advantages? Would it be possible to create an uncontested market space?

In short, most strategic discussions turn into the adoption of conventional strategy thinking according to which you have to choose between different generic strategies. However, in numerous competitive and hypercompetitive environments you may eventually fail, if you either continue differentiating your products and services or if you keep lowering your price.

We have worked both in practice and in theory to turn the conventional wisdom on its head. Instead of being stuck in the middle between differentiation and cost leadership, could you, strategically, view this Gordian Knot as a hidden opportunity? Can you untie the Gordian Knot and realize both the benefit of differentiation and cost leadership at one and the same time?

Gradually, we began to uncover this opportunity when dealing with the notion and business realities of ***discount strategy***, which is grossly overlooked in the literature on management and strategy. We hope that you will find the insights on crafting and executing discount strategies relevant and useful – perhaps from a theoretical perspective in order to brush up the conventional thinking, perhaps from the perspective of inventing and executing a discount strategy yourself, or maybe you are just a conventional incumbent who would like to be in the forefront of the battle against competitors adopting a discount strategy.

Welcome to the battlefield of discount!

It is never a battle to write a book on the battles of business, but it may be a struggle from time to time. Any acknowledgement in this book should therefore in the first place go to those individuals who helped us overcome headwind. A special thank you goes to Morten Froholdt who undertook research responsibilities and even at one stage took on some stewardship in order to accelerate the progress of the work and to Kathrine Høeg and Helle Moesgaard Andersen for applying their eagle eyes in polishing the final manuscript.

A special thank you goes to the editors Francesca Warren and Jo Golesworthy, both of John Wiley & Sons, for supporting the endeavor of transforming our ideas and experiences into a book.

And we also offer many thanks to business individuals interviewed as part of our research and colleagues with whom we have had many stimulating conversations on strategy and discount business models. A special thank you goes to our families. Although they did not always understand that sitting behind a computer through the night can be exciting and rewarding they provided us with a lot of support and encouragement.

Finally, we are also grateful to those companies who are sharing the same belief; that dealing with discount strategy offers radically new insights as to how some companies will be successful while the ignorance of others may make them fall behind.

Michael Moesgaard Andersen and Flemming Poulfelt
Copenhagen
28 February 2006

1

Why are some companies more successful than others?

The real life laboratory

Undoubtedly, strategy is important and it is described in the management literature, in management consulting, and in practical stewardship in private and public companies. Invariably, an aspiration for the adoption of the 'right' strategy prevails.

However, is it true that there is such a thing as the one and only best strategy for a company? Is the market leader of today the industry winner of tomorrow? Is it possible to create sustainable competitive advantage simply by way of adopting a generic strategy? Can you, generally, craft a strategy to create uncontested market space and thereby make the competition irrelevant?

In a world constantly in search of rationalism, it would be nice, if we were able to give the straightforward answer 'yes'.

However, we think that the answer to each question is probably 'no'. When we say probably it is because you should never exclude the possibility that new empirical findings could lead to new insights.

Over the past two decades alone, strategic analyses and books searching for the keys to high performance have included *In Search of Excellence* published in 1982 [1], *Corporate Culture and Performance* from 1992 [2], *Build to Last* from 1994 [3], through to the more recent *Good to Great* [4], *What Really Works* [5] and *Blue Ocean Strategy* [6] published in 2001, 2003 and 2005 respectively. The question within strategic management remains the same, namely 'What is the most successful strategy?' But the answers offered in the literature appear to be many and varied.

Michael Porter's conventional wisdom from the early 80s recommends that you should choose between a differentiator type of strategy or become a cost leader. In recent strategic literature Kim and Mauborgne in *Blue Ocean Strategy* [6] tell you to create uncontested market space and simply make the competition irrelevant. In *What Really Works* [5], Joyce, Nohria and Roberson develop a model known as the 4+2 model as a recipe for success. This model is based on a thorough analysis and argues that focus on four key areas coupled with an additional two areas chosen from a possible four should lead to superior performance.

One of the problems with many of the normative strategy schools is that they cannot adequately explain why winners emerge in hypercompetitive markets. On the one hand, it is about creating superior value and, on the the other, it might be about developing value destruction. However, the notion of value destruction is explored less as a consequence of a strategy aiming to create value. Surely, many are familiar with creative destruction as described by Schumpeter [7] but what if the value destruction doesn't stem from new and improved technology or products alone but also from new and different strategies?

All industries may then be at risk in terms of the potential value destruction lurking in an unknown future. This risk, or opportunity, is precisely the reason for this book and its focus on exploring why some companies are more successful than others. Or rather why some companies successfully bridge the gap between differentiator and cost leader type of strategies and emerge as winners in hypercompetitive markets and what this entails in terms of value destruction and creation.

Creating value and simultaneous destruction

The majority of managers think in traditional terms in which a product is produced at a cost and sold at a margin. This approach is regarded as creating value for the customer in some sense and value for the owner or shareholder to take home. This rather simple concept of business is expressed by the founder of the Body Shop Anita Roddick who states that [8]:

> Business is not financial science, it's about trading . . . buying and selling. It's about creating a product or service so good that people will pay for it.

Now what about creating a product or service, which is good enough for people to use but is free of charge? Is that good business sense, financial science or just plain lunacy? Some would cry out 'madness' while others such as the two founders of Skype, would describe it as good business sense. Such good sense that it has resulted in the sale of Skype to eBay for US$2.6 billion only three years after the first user downloaded the Skype software from the Internet.

When pondering what eBay has actually purchased, the immediate answer that it has bought an IP telephone operator appears to be far from the truth as it has bought a company which can provide an added benefit for the users of eBay. As such, Skype is viewed by eBay as an extension of its existing business by extending the Internet infrastructure of eBay with IP telephony. This means that the customers can not only communicate by e-mail but they can also speak to each other at a very competitive rate!

Regardless of eBay's intentions, US$2.6 billion has been created for the shareholders of Skype over the past three years along with an overwhelming potential for value destruction across the entire industry of telephone communications. The usage per minute charges of the traditional telecommunications industry are seriously at risk from the free telephony offered to users of Skype who are calling other Skype users.

One reason for this value destruction is technological development and the fact that many Internet connections can support telephony. It is, however, not the only reason as the possibility of Internet telephony has been known for a long time and has been attempted by others. So what is the secret behind the huge success of Skype?

Clear focus and exceptional execution of a discount strategy can be argued to be the main reasons for Skype's success as opposed to, e.g. proprietary technology. A discount strategy of such magnitude may alter the nature of the telecommunications industry. The chairman of the Federal Communications Commission is in fact convinced that not only will Skype change the industry but also the world of communications (Fortune Magazine, February 16, 2004):

> I knew it was over when I downloaded Skype, Michael Powell, chairman, Federal Communications Commission, explained. When the inventors of KaZaA are distributing for free a little program that you can use to talk to anybody else, and the quality is fantastic, and it's free – it's over. The world will change now inevitably.

The founders of Skype had little doubt that the telecommunications industry was about to change and that a value destruction across the traditional providers would be a result of this, as the following quote from Niklas Zennstöm, CEO and co-founder of Skype, shows clearly:

> The idea of charging for calls belongs to the last century. Skype software gives people new power to affordably stay in touch with their friends and family by taking advantage of their technology and connectivity investments.

There is little doubt that technological developments acted as a catalyst for Skype but other more traditional industries have also been exposed to companies who turn things upside down. Companies who create value for themselves while developing the destruction of value for others.

IKEA is one of the more traditional companies which have changed the industry and signalled value destruction for the traditional furniture manufacturers operating in the 1970's. However, this was not due to technological innovation but merely a result of a vision and a strategy devised by the now legendary founder of IKEA, Ingvar Kamprad [9].

> We shall offer a wide range of home furnishing items of good design and function at prices so low that the majority of people can afford to buy them . . . We have great ambitions.

The value created for IKEA and the value destruction this entailed for its competitors was not due to technical innovation but merely to a different way of approaching the market. Is there anything in common between these two companies that can be identified as key factors for their success? Judging by the amount of daily Skype downloads, and the vision of Ingvar Kamprad, volume appears to hold some significance.

The volume game

As not all companies can create value through offering a product or service free of charge, they seek to price it low and make up for this lower margin through volume.

When IKEA opened near Munich in 1974, West Germany was Europe's largest market as well as the largest producer and exporter of furniture. At that time the German furniture retail industry consisted of retailers who were using showrooms, taking orders from manufacturers which resulted in limited inventories leading to long delivery times. IKEA did it differently. They promised low prices, immediate delivery and Swedish quality and 37,000 people visited the store during the first three days.

Despite vigorous responses from German retailers, IKEA and their low cost concept were there to stay and by the late 1970's they had captured a 50 % share of the West German cash-and-carry segment. Today IKEA has locations from Iceland to Kuwait covering all continents, their catalogue has been printed in more copies than the Bible and endless hordes of people are passing through their stores on a daily basis.

The American company Costco is another company which has been instrumental in reshaping the retail industry and looking for high volumes rather than high margins. With a company policy stating that the mark-up of goods may not rise above 14 %, high volumes have been essential in recording annual net sales of more than US$ 40 billion [10].

The sheer size of this volume is further emphasized by the fact that one in four American households holds a membership of Costco [11]. The combination of such volume and the ceiling on mark-ups has had serious consequences for the retail industry as a whole as Costco may not only be cheaper but also reaches a phenomenal number of customers. This customer base has been achieved over the past two decades by breaking the traditional mold of not only retailing but also of strategy making in general.

Volume is the essence of Skype and its impact is not in doubt but the increase in number of downloads since the first software was made available to the public is astounding. Since day one, Skype has maintained its rate of downloads resulting in more than 200 million people who have downloaded the Skype software up to 2005. Looking solely at the American market, research shows that Skype accounts for a large percentage of the IP current telephony (analysis done by broadband management company Sandvine Inc):

Calls using Skype Technologies SA account for nearly half of the VOIP minutes used (46.2 percent) and about 40 percent of the VOIP bandwidth used in North America.

In addition to the above it should be noted that Skype achieved one billion minutes of Skype-to-Skype usage in 2004, one year after they made their downloadable software available. In 2005 this figure had climbed to 10 billion Skype-to-Skype minutes which, when illustrated in Figure 1.1, shows an astonishing trend.

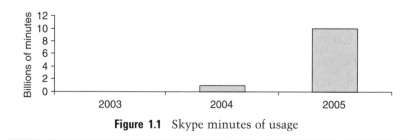

Figure 1.1 Skype minutes of usage

If this trend continues the question becomes whether Skype will reach 100 billion in 2006? Imagine that: 100 billion minutes of free Skype-to-Skype minutes which were previously offered by traditional telecommunications companies at a monopolistic charge. Even if that charge, on average, is assumed to be as low as US$ 0.01, Skype would be causing a value destruction of US$ 1 billion due to high volume.

By comparison, AT&T Communication and MCI WorldCom each recorded approximately 20 billion minutes of international traffic in 2003 [12]. Skype has already grown to half the size of these two operators of international traffic, which is quite an achievement in just two years.

Clearly, volume is instrumental in succeeding with a low price product but is that the only explanation? Low price and high volume? Perhaps, but how to make such a business model work?

How does a company play the high volume, low price game whilst at the same time ensuring that it stands out from its competitors? Is it at all possible to pursue a low cost strategy and differentiation at the same time?

It appears so and not just through inventing new industries, or new markets, which can be considered 'Blue Oceans' in the short-term, but through changing the unwritten laws. This sounds like a complex managerial assignment. However, in this context, there is a need for making things simple. Therefore, simplicity can not be underestimated in the process of succeeding with such a strategy.

Simplicity – the word of the day

A simple message is easier to convey than a complex one.

Simplicity, however, seems also to be the generic theme of many emerging winners in hypercompetitive industries who are seemingly following the condemned strategy of 'Stuck in the middle'. Not only simplicity in how they communicate to the consumers through ads and campaigns but also the simplicity of the product, the supporting of such, internal processes and even down to the lay-out of, e.g. a retail outlet.

How can such simplicity create winners when traditional thinking on differentiation has worked on making products more complicated by enhancing product variations or the services surrounding them? Has this kind of thinking been overestimated or is it just wrong? Neither, as it still works for some. Perhaps too much emphasis has been put on traditional thinking even though other ways would have proven just as successful or in some cases even more successful.

In many places the traditional way of acquiring a telephone line may take some time and in some cases even include the necessity of subscribing to a specific provider. With Skype, free software is downloaded, installed on a PC, plugged into a headset and then you can call other Skype users. For an additional fee non Skype users can be called at prices significantly lower than those offered by traditional providers. Simple indeed and by keeping the very product simple, the administration and back-office processes required to support this should also be simple or simplified. Communicating a simple offer is also easier and leaves more room for the message to actually stick with the customer, as opposed to the increasing number of businesses who are attempting to stand-out with an offer as complex as the one offered by a competitor.

Offering a simple, or simpler, product was one of the main reasons for the success of IKEA as they redefined the industry with furniture manufactured for self-assembly.

As such, a simple product which the customers can assemble themselves enabled instant delivery as the furniture could be stored at the warehouse in flat pack boxes. Not only did this suit the buyers of home furniture, who, prior to IKEA, had to wait weeks for that new sofa or shelf system, but it also lowered the costs borne by IKEA. This allowed IKEA to not only operate at a lower cost but also provided the opportunity to differentiate their offer from the traditional furniture manufacturers.

Costco may not produce simple products but they hold a limited number of articles in their stores compared to, e.g. supermarkets. This leads to simpler processes and systems and therefore lower costs. One could on the back of this fear that the experience of the customer would be diminished by this but apparently the customers of Costco are satisfied, judged by the vast number of members.

This may be due to the fact that they know exactly what Costco is about, large quantities at low prices across a limited selection of articles whereas other retailers are finding it hard to position themselves in the competitive arena. Some are offering an endless amount of goods causing the customer to search aisle after aisle trying to find a pound of sugar or a pint of milk while being distracted by imaginative shop-in-shops or promotional displays.

Simplicity as described above comes in many guises ranging from the product itself to the communication of what value it has for potential buyers. As such it is not a single quick fix of simplifying the product line but perhaps the ability to adopt simplicity as a code encompassing all areas of the business.

Once such a philosophy is adopted throughout the organization it appears that products or services can be offered at a lower cost. Furthermore, the simple nature of the product seems to sit well with consumers as they relish such simplicity as a fresh injection of something that is easy to comprehend.

The mantra is simple then: 'keep it simple' and be true to the chosen path of simplicity. The real world however, may be slightly more complex because what is simple? What is a simple product? Or how do you simplify the product that is already there as IKEA, Costco and Skype have done?

Cut to the core

The notion of a simple product is in fact simple. It revolves around what the customer's actual need is when buying a product. This sounds rather straight forward but when dwelling on this thought and some of the products we all buy, what exact need are we trying to fulfil? When buying telephony are the customers satisfying only their need for voice communication or are they looking to satisfy some need of security through the established quality of traditional fixed line telephony? When buying a sofa are the customers trying to satisfy their need to sit comfortably or the need to decorate their living room aesthetically? When entering a retail outlet are the customers trying to satisfy their need to find the items on their list or are they looking to satisfy the need for a shopping experience and if so what is that?

This line of thought could be extended further for quite some time and offers numerous arguments concerning what needs various goods are looking to fulfil. However, instead of venturing down that path towards complexity we will keep it simple.

Skype is offering very inexpensive voice communication and nothing else. They do not guarantee that your Skype connection is infallible or offer trendy headsets in the light blue colours of Skype. In fact, they offer you a program you can use to call via the Internet and nothing more, which it is argued is the core of voice communication: to enable the customer to communicate with someone else located elsewhere.

The case of IKEA is perhaps better suited to illustrating this point as they do not make furniture according to specification or furniture with complex carving and ornamentation. They make, e.g. simple tables, chairs, sofas and shelf systems which fulfil the needs of the customers: to furnish their homes at a reasonable price. In addition to the simple design of their furniture, IKEA lets the customers collect their items at the warehouse and obliges them to assemble the pieces themselves. The entire value proposition is simple: you look, you decide, you collect and you pay for exactly what is in the box whether it is a table, chair or sofa – and nothing else.

Costco has, like Skype and IKEA, managed to differentiate itself from the competition by stripping all unnecessary evils out of the shopping experience. As such it holds a limited range of articles, which customers will find presented in bulk format and which they may need to unwrap as no unnecessary shop assistants are employed solely for the purpose of unwrapping goods and arranging them on limited shelf space.

This 'cutting to the core' is concerned with stripping the product or offering it in such a way that it meets, and even exceeds, the need of the customer. This notion is some- what contradictory to the literature concerning relationship marketing and service management, which has increased over the past two decades. Both are areas which add to the possi- bilities of differentiation.

The notion of providing the customer with exactly what he or she wants is, however, far from novel. Nor is the importance of volume or the fact that such products have the potential of creating high volume sales:

> A market is never saturated with a good product, but it is very quickly saturated with a bad one.

> Henry Ford

As Henry Ford rightly puts it, a good product will have a demand attached to it but is the product of our emerging winners necessarily a good product in a traditional sense? Does it offer higher quality than those of the competitor? Does it do something that the competitor's products can't do? Not necessarily, but this may not be required as long as the customer perceives this product as offering a higher value.

One area that has been explored by Skype, IKEA and Costco is the idea of self-service. Such an idea would have been unheard of in the days of traditional telephony, furniture sales and retail but has been instrumental in how these companies have been perceived by the customer.

Service? Something we'd rather do ourselves

When was the last time you were put on hold or forced to listen to dubious music while waiting for your local service representative to retrieve your details? Perhaps you waited for a printed airline ticket to arrive in the mail, growing evermore concerned that it may not arrive and that your holiday to the Bahamas was at risk? These concerns or inconveniences are drastically reduced if there is no need to call for assistance or be at the mercy of a printed ticket, arriving by mail.

So, in conjunction with cutting to the core, it seems that the emerging winners have all introduced self-service in industries where this to some extent was unheard of.

When viewing your Skype account, you log on to your own page and view those details without the assistance of a service representative, which means that you have access to real time information whenever you want it. No more waiting on hold or being transferred back and forth between departments because you are performing the service yourself. The installation of the software required is equally up to you as an individual customer, as well as ensuring that your connection and system meets the requirements.

IKEA is a classic example of self-service where the customers are given access to the warehouse in order for them to pick their chosen furniture, which is found in flat pack boxes. One can only imagine the reaction of traditional furniture producers when this concept was launched in the early 1970's.

This, however, enhanced the customers' perception of service as they could walk through the show room, choose their furniture, go and pick it up at the warehouse and literally be able to change their entire living room in one day.

Therefore, a high level of service may no longer be measured by the number of services but rather the ability to include the customer in the production of services. Who can claim they have received a poor service when they have performed it themselves?

This self-service and the other areas described previously are some of the areas that we argue have been instrumental in the success of our winners and their ability to redefine the industries in which they compete. While being instrumental these described areas also contradict with traditional strategic thinking.

The black box of strategy turned upside down

Value destruction, cost leadership and differentiation are often co-existing. The important thing is to get back to the core and to service as something the customer produces. All seem to contradict traditional strategy thinking.

We argue that the black box of strategy with its current thinking lacks the tools and ideas to explain the phenomenon of how companies emerge as winners in hypercompetitive industries.

In our research, therefore, we have focused on how companies can gain a foothold in hypercompetitive markets and how they can be successful. We have been studying various companies in various markets and in the book we explore in detail the reasons and explanations for their success. Based upon our general observations and three in depth case analyses we outline and develop a framework for how to create and execute discount business strategies. Through this we also add and describe some new dimensions of strategy both in theory and in practice.

2

The oxymoron of existing strategies: where do we go from here?

Conventional strategic thinking

Many strategic thinkers have fostered normative strategy road maps, and have tried consistently to demonstrate that one strategy is better than another. In other words, an apparent oxymoron exists, as it amounts to a misunderstanding to combine two generic strategies and, if executed at all, a business case based on an oxymoron would fail. Consequently, we shall investigate the oxymoron syndrome of existing business strategies theoretically as well as empirically and help mitigate some of the serious loopholes in existing business strategy theories.

With his prescriptive models of a company's path to obtaining and sustaining competitive advantage, Michael E. Porter has been one of the most influential contributors to the field of strategic management in the past two decades. Born out of the field of economics and industrial organization, Porter has emphasized the level of industry profitability as the most significant factor affecting a firm's profitability, and likewise posited that the strategy creation process can be simplified to a point where it is a matter of *choosing* the proper strategy as opposed to *crafting* the proper strategy.

For a number of reasons, we aim to challenge one of Porter's pivotal ideas pertaining to the existence of two universally applicable *generic* strategies, which have been made part of the fundamental theoretical toolbox for managers and business students worldwide, and which constitute today almost irrefutable 'laws of nature' within strategic management. While the ideas were first published more than 25 years ago, it is still regarded as detrimental to a company's success to pursue both a *differentiation* and a *cost-leadership* strategy.

Thus, we propose a simple yet highly controversial question: Can a differentiated cost-leader, the oxymoron, succeed in a highly competitive market?

The generic strategy framework

As outlined above, there are essentially two basic strategies that a firm can pursue. It must either choose to become a cost-leader, which entails a rigorous pursuit of efficiency and economies of scale in the sourcing and production processes in order to achieve a competitive advantage.

Or a company can do the opposite and differentiate its products or services – either functionally or perceptively – to achieve a higher margin per output by increasing the buyer's value from acquiring the product. Furthermore, by pursuing either of the strategies within a narrowly defined market segment, the company can opt to adopt a third generic strategy – namely one of *focus*. In this sense, as illustrated below, the focus strategies are regarded essentially as subsets of the two primary generic strategies of cost leadership and differentiation: see Figure 2.1.

Thus, as opposed to being faced with a multitude of different options when conceiving strategic plans, managers effectively find themselves in a trilemma when attempting to steer their companies towards sustained profitability. Should a manager fail to acknowledge this and make the critical error of pursuing more than one of these strategies, a firm risks becoming 'stuck

	Lower Cost	Differentiation
Broad Market	1. Cost Leadership	2. Differentiation
Narrow Market	3A. Cost Focus	3B. Differentiation Focus

Figure 2.1 Porter's generic strategies [1]. Reprinted with the permission of The Free Press, a Division of Simon & Schuster Adult Publishing Group, from Competitive Advantage: Creating and Sustaining Superior Performance by Michael E. Porter. Copyright © 1985, 1998 by Michael E. Porter. All Rights Reserved

in the middle', which is the worst position conceivable – as Porter puts it: *'Being "all things to all people" is a recipe for strategic mediocrity and below-average performance.'* [2]

With its simplicity inarguably adding to its popularity, the generic strategy framework has been widely accepted as a good fundamental guideline for strategic managers. Moreover, research has been put forward to assess the validity of the framework, and in fact, several scientific studies have indicated that firms pursuing clear-cut generic strategies tend to consistently outperform those that do not.

One study concluded, while conceding the fact that the specific industry environment affects the applicability of the respective generic strategies, that Porter's typology apparently helps in the identification of the highly profitable players within an industry [3]. Subsequently, another study was conducted by employing the paints manufacturing industry as basis for the analysis, and included concrete interpretations of the implications of pursuing a specific generic strategy as identified by a panel of industry experts.

The outcome was reported enthusiastically by the researchers: Firms with one generic strategy type outperformed firms identified as 'stuck in the middle' [4]. Finally, a diligent statistical analysis of the competitive advantage of business service firms has likewise suggested that Porter's generic strategies are in fact indicative of performance levels [5].

Invariably, such strong empirical justification galvanizes the appealing nature of Porter's generic strategies, leaving room for what could be called the Porter's fan club.

Porter challenged

Despite the widespread enthusiasm for Porter's generic strategies, some critics have voiced opinions that may point towards important deficiencies and limitations in this paradigm. Firstly, it is a primary focus of criticism that Porter is too concerned with the narrow context of established big businesses. Mature and saturated industries are prioritized over niche and fragmented ones, and this obviously imposes certain limitations upon the (supposedly universally applicable) generic strategy framework. While it is clear that Porter's research is very much founded on hard data, which is naturally easier to obtain in mature industries, there is some indication that his framework cannot be applied reliably to more dynamic and evolving industries [6].

Secondly, critics have argued that any application of a generic strategy is subject to a host of environment-specific conditions that will have a significant effect upon the profitability associated with the chosen strategy. Thus, in effect the generic strategy framework is far too *simplistic* and *deterministic* to fully capture the complex problems that managers are facing when they attempt to craft winning strategies. Moreover, with the generic approach the company will invariably end up copying other players in its market, which can only lead to average performance. After all, if one does the same as one's competitors, one can at best hope to become the equal of one's competitors – never to beat them.

Criticism is likewise manifested in a number of statistical and anecdotal arguments demonstrating significant flaws and inconsistencies in the generic strategy framework. For example, a study in 1986 was constructed on the hypothesis that the applicability of Porter's typology is very much dependent on the industry focused upon. Thus, the consumer durables industry was examined further and, in two separate studies, it was confirmed empirically that:

A. Porter's typology cannot fully capture the characteristics of the firms in this industry. In effect, differentiators also employed elements of a cost-leadership strategy and the cost-leaders employed significant elements of differentiation [7].

B. Superior performance was invariably linked to the possession of strategic advantages, but there was little or no indication that having strategic advantages that pertained to more than one of the generic strategies would lead to inferior performance. In other words, strict adherence to one generic strategy did not necessarily imply success [8].

Other strategy researchers have expressed criticism of Porter's approach, described broadly as the positioning school, which they view as overly restricted [9]. In the context of our approach, the most relevant criticism is that Porter is very much concerned with 'choosing' the 'right' strategy as opposed to inducing and inventing novel strategy. A strategy is not crafted, it is chosen. Looking at strategy from such a static perspective, there is the risk of overlooking the fact that success in competitive environments often requires ongoing processes, dynamic intervention, organization building and people development.

Ironically, Porter deals with generic strategies in the context of competitive environments whereas they may be more relevant in non-competitive environments.

Subsequent to the studies and the theoretical criticism from the academics, empirically founded criticism has also been expressed. In particular, emphasis has been placed on identifying companies that did not match the generic strategy framework and using this as a means for deriving a more generalized rule vis-à-vis the applicability of the framework.

A pertinent example of this is Seven Eleven – the branded drug store found on many street corners in the western hemisphere. Whether or not Seven Eleven pursues a differentiator or a cost-leader strategy is difficult to say. Indeed, if compared with the local drug stores, gas stations etc., Seven Eleven is clearly a cost-leader, as the company's magnitude and superior logistics afford it a competitive advantage via economics of scale. However, if compared with the major supermarket chains, with whom Seven Eleven likewise competes, the company is clearly differentiated on parameters such as convenience, long hours, etc. Thus, Seven Eleven has successfully employed both elements of a cost-leader and elements of a differentiator type of strategy – it is merely a matter of which part of the competitive scene is used for comparison [10].

The example of Proctor & Gamble in the diapers industry is also illustrative in this context. P&G first launched its *Pampers* brand in 1966 and thus changed the strategic rules within the industry as these constituted the first disposable diapers on the market.

Meanwhile, although at first a product differentiation strategy was employed, P&G has managed to shift its strategic focus from differentiation to cost-leadership (via its highly efficient production apparatus) and back – depending always on the strategies of the competition faced at any given point in time. Thus, the P&G case is an apt illustration of how the generic strategy framework does not capture the dynamic perspective and the possibility of altering strategic focus should industry conditions demand it [11].

Finally, the beer industry has been highlighted as an example of an industry where customers appreciate an attractive brand image, and high quality, but also a reasonable price. This, in turn, accounts for the success of companies such as Anheuser-Busch, which has combined cost and quality to offer a superior product. Clearly, various imported labels are more differentiated, and various local brands are cheaper, but the Missouri based brewer has positioned itself successfully with a value proposition that, according to Porter, would get the company 'stuck in the middle' [12].

Mixed strategies – the airline industry

While the evidence contests the universal applicability of Porter's generic strategy framework, a certain gap remains in business literature regarding whether or not a concrete strategy configuration can be identified that will allow a company to pursue both a differentiation and a cost-leadership strategy simultaneously. The airline industry is a good illustration in this context with regard to both the initial applicability of Porter's generic strategies and the fact that these have subsequently lost their relevance.

In 1981 the Scandinavian Airlines System (SAS) introduced a new segmentation envisaged as a new 'Euro Class', where the standard of service was raised significantly with more space, a gourmet dinner with real cutlery, fast check-in, extra careful baggage handling, various in-flight services, advanced lounge service, elaborate bonus air-mile collection schemes, etc aimed deliberately to prevent passengers choosing not to go 'Euro Class'. This trend was soon followed by a considerable number of other flag-carriers.

However, SAS was the airline which developed this concept to its extreme, repainting the aircraft, training the service staff to smile even more, and awarding extra benefits to the 'Euro Class' passenger.

Moreover, SAS went on to exploit its service image within catering, and they also joined forces with Radisson in order to deliver hotel services to its customers, who could therefore hardly avoid an extreme degree of service before, during and after air travel. SAS had become a swan in the service business and was no longer a simple airborne carrier.

This simultaneous combination of segmentation and service attracted considerable attention in the 80's, as illustrated by Richard Normann with his focus on *Service Management – Strategy and Leadership in Service Business* [13]. Strategists soon learned that the airline industry had created an extended and refined version of Porter's differentiator type of strategy.

The philosophy behind it was to distinguish between the *core services* (the flight from A to B) and the *peripheral services* [14]. Today, 'peripheral services' is almost a forgotten term in the strategy literature being substituted with what Kotler has called the *augmented product*: see Figure 2.2.

However, peripheral services and augmented products are essentially the same.

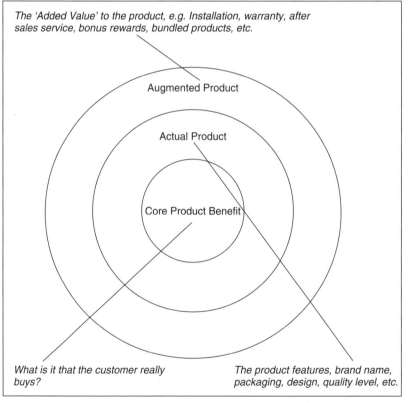

Figure 2.2 Illustration of Kotler's augmented product [15]. Kotler, Philip, Armstrong, Gary, Principles of Marketing and Student DVD PKG, 10th Edition, © 2004. Adapted by permission of Pearson Education, Inc., Upper Saddle River, NJ

As SAS and other similar service companies grew successful, core services became less important and peripheral services – or Kotler's augmented products, if you like – became extremely important under the banner of giving the customers an exceptional service. The rationale behind this line of thinking was that an exceptional (peripheral) service would make the airline deliver to the customer at a level over and above expectations, or – as Richard Normann puts it – '*It takes 12 pluses to make up for a single minus*' [16].

When the service provider and the service customer meet, we have *the moment of truth* or where the rubber meets the road. Or, illustrating the importance of the customer relations: 'A large service company may well experience thousands of "moments of truth" every day'. Consequently, the ideal strategy of the firm is to deliver as much service, in particular peripheral services, as it possibly can [17].

The service strategy as an extended version of Porter's differentiation strategy proved highly successful for the airline carriers throughout the 80's. The success of SAS therefore seemed to galvanize the generic strategies and furthermore refine his differentiation strategy by way of a service strategy, focusing on peripheral services and every day's moment of truth.

However, the competitive advantage of flag-carriers based on a differentiated service strategy soon disappeared in the second half of the 90's when the discount carriers emerged. Some businesses were geared to provide an aggressively priced product while maintaining a high level of differentiation on a number of key parameters. Consider examples such as easyJet, Ryanair and Go, which clearly provided the lowest priced product on account of their cost leadership, but likewise managed to maintain a position as the airlines with the most reliable flight schedule (arrival and departure times), the most convenient ticketing process and a high rating on the customer service scale. As subsequent sections will demonstrate, Ryanair is only one of many examples of this apparent oxymoron, and a greater understanding of these companies' strategic efforts is called for.

In fact, Ryanair is not differentiated when using the conventional definition of the term among incumbent airlines. In the mid 90's when Ryanair's strategy started to have a real impact, the major airlines had been differentiating themselves for decades on various configurations of the peripheral or augmented product features.

Thus, with a highly commoditized product, it is obviously impossible to differentiate an offering on the core product benefit. When somebody purchases an airline ticket, they purchase the fast, physical relocation of themselves for a certain period of time – nothing more, nothing less. However, with an array of peripheral or augmented product features, the high end airlines had been competing for ages to provide the best package of non-essential product features to achieve differentiation priced at a significant premium.

While these features were growing and increasingly accepted as *minimum product standards* within the industry, Ryanair contested the underlying question as to whether these services were relevant to the majority of the flying population when considering the substantial savings that could be derived from eliminating them. The company was right. As will be elaborated further in Chapter 6, Ryanair implemented a *discount* strategy and successfully slashed its peripheral and augmented product features. In turn, the company focused on re-channeling the resources that were made available – partly towards substantial price reductions and partly towards the points of differentiation that made a *real* difference to buyers (e.g. whether or not the plane arrives on time.) In this sense, Ryanair can even be said to have disrupted the airline industry.

Initially, we thought that the notion of blue ocean strategy could explain and foster the theoretical background for Ryanair's and similar companies' success by its focus on value innovation and its dismissal of conventional strategy:

> It is conventionally believed that companies can either create greater value to customers at a higher cost or create reasonable value at a lower cost. Here strategy is seen as making choice between differentiation and low cost. In contrast, those that seek to create blue oceans pursue differentiation and low cost simultaneously [18].

However, the focus on blue ocean strategy is *'how to create uncontested market space and make competition irrelevant'* (the subtitle of the *Blue Ocean Strategy* book), whereas Ryanair and many others are precisely in the opposite market space, namely the hypercompetitive market. This is also true, in practice, for all other companies pursuing discount strategies.

Not surprisingly, Ryanair and similar cases are not addressed in Kim and Mauborgne's *Blue Ocean Strategy*, whereas, e.g. Virgin Atlantic Airways' Upper Class brand is addressed [19], sharing similar characteristics with SAS's Euro Class segmentation strategy in the 80's.

Notwithstanding all the hallmarks of the blue ocean strategy, this shows that it differs widely from the discount strategy (including its wider repercussions) developed in this book.

One way to illustrate this is summarized in Figure 2.3 which at the same time positions the discount strategy against the generic strategies.

With the airline industry as one case in point, it can be concluded that neither the generic strategies nor the blue ocean strategy can explain or provide a guide as to how discount has been adopted so successfully. Later in the book we shall investigate the core elements of the discount strategy further, not only in the airline industry but also in other competitive market spaces such as the mobile communications business and the retail grocery industry.

Generic Strategies	Blue Oceans Strategy	Discount Strategy
Compete in existing market space	Create uncontested market space	Compete in hypercompetitive market space
Beat the competitors	Make the competition irrelevant	Own value creation while destructing of value for others
Exploit existing demand	Create and capture new demand	Both supply push and demand pull
Choose either differentiation or cost leadership	Create (uncontested) value	Craft the strategy with disruptive effect

Figure 2.3 Comparative assessment of the main strategies

Rather than formulating a theoretical piece of strategy deductively we shall investigate some cases in considerable depth in order to assess the trajectory of a discount strategy, to explore the development of such a strategy and thereafter to (inductively) assess the likely wider repercussions of this strategic approach.

Much attention has been attracted to the notion of value creation, and the discount strategy also addresses this aspect. However, it should be taken into account that a successful discount strategy also implies value destruction: cf. Figure 2.4.

Value destruction is one of the elements which are not addressed directly in the literature on business strategy. But this is not the only element. A properly crafted discount strategy inherits various elements which shall be explored later in the book.

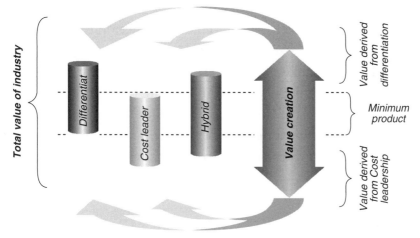

Figure 2.4 Illustration of value creation and value destruction

In addition, the concept, as such, of a discount strategy has not been the subject of much attention in the business literature, if addressed at all.

One conclusion may be drawn already at this stage and that has to do with the fact that the conventional oxymoron seems to wither away under the aegis of a discount strategy. This is illustrated by the fact that discount strategies deal with differentiation and cost leadership at the same time, thereby making the choice of one of the generic strategies irrelevant. Moreover, the new blue ocean oxymoron – that you should make the competition irrelevant in a world of ever increasing competition and create uncontested market space even in hypercompetitive markets – is contested by a discount strategy, which is based on a hypercompetitive market and on the value that the market space is contestable at all times.

The oxymoron of the conventional generic strategies appears to be dead in the discount strategy.

Having now set the scene with an introduction to the empirically emerging discount strategies, we shall employ more detailed case analyses in the next chapters in order to provide an exploration of the process of moving from either Porter's generic strategies or Kim and Mauborgne's blue ocean strategy over to discount strategy. Later we will deal with both the construction of the discount strategy as well as the aspects of execution.

3

When discount strategy becomes important

Hyper competitive markets and traditional strategy

The possibility of differentiating on the core of a commoditized product itself is very limited, if it exists at all. This has supported the idea of peripheral services as a vehicle, which would allow a company to differentiate itself despite competing in an industry of commodities. The traditional approach of choosing either to differentiate or to become a cost leader has embraced this idea as it allowed for some differentiation and the notion of charging a premium price even within hyper competitive markets where the core product could be argued to resemble a commodity.

The effect of this has been a continuous search along two dimensions of competitive parameters. These two dimensions are the perceived product performance and the price, or costs when relating back to the generic strategies. As can be seen from Figure 3.1 these two dimensions have traditionally been linked together in such a way that an increase in product performance would trigger an increase in price/costs and vice versa.

Restricted by the notion that the two dimensions are mutually exclusive and that a strategy based on both cannot be executed due to the risk of being stuck in the middle, strategies in a traditional sense will plot somewhere along the dotted line. Given that competitors seek mainly to differentiate themselves on similar parameters, such as quality, exceptional customer service or loyalty programs, the competitive arena and their strategies can be depicted by the circled area.

Pairing this with a hyper competitive market, where numerous competitors battle fiercely for a share of the spoils, leads to a potential situation where all players in a given

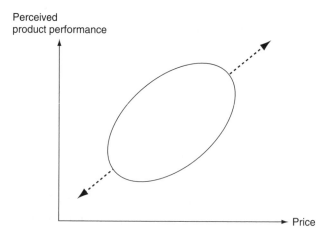

Figure 3.1 Traditional strategy on two dimensions

industry attempt to position themselves within the boundaries of the traditional strategy sphere.

When all players are 'choosing' their strategy in such a manner, is it then possible for the individual customer to differentiate all these value propositions, that are based on either of two dimensions?

The answer would lean towards a 'no' because if all competitors are attempting to differentiate themselves on, e.g. specific peripheral services common to the industry, they are in fact aligning themselves with each other. This leaves the customer with a highly contested market where it is hard to distinguish the various competitors from each other as they all appear to be offering the same.

The idea of competing on and developing specific peripheral services common to the industry follows from the analogies between technological sophistication and the development of peripheral or augmented product features. Rather than technical innovations, traditional competitors are in a sense innovating their peripheral product features in order to increase their margins along a trajectory of increased perceived product performance. This, however, is in many instances based on what was previously available in the market, and what the customer is expected to want.

Strategy in a traditional sense will therefore, when applied to a hyper competitive market, lead to a large amount of competitors attempting to differentiate themselves along a similar set of variables. The result invariably becomes a highly competitive market where all companies are quite similar and little differentiation is apparent.

This situation is equal to what Kim and Mauborgne describe as a 'Red Ocean' where numerous competitors inhabit the waters competing fiercely for a chunk of each other's market share.

The question is therefore: how can a company break the mold and truly differentiate its offering during the ongoing competition? As previously discussed, the traditional approach has been to continuously develop peripheral services on top of a commoditized core product. Kim and Mauborgne argue that completely new market spaces must be developed in order to steer clear of these 'Red Oceans' in search of 'Blue Oceans' characterized by an uncontested market space.

As the latter may be short-lived if at all possible, another approach is that of a discount strategy where the traditional boundaries for strategic thinking are challenged and elements of both a differentiator and cost leader strategy are utilized. Such an approach seeks to effectively position a company outside the space occupied by the traditional competitors while still competing in a 'Red Ocean' context.

The position of a discount strategy

In an overcrowded market space where competition in a traditional sense would be to differentiate the offering through a sustained development of peripheral services, the discount approach moves in the opposite direction.

Rooted in the fact that the core product can be characterized as a commodity, the discount approach seeks ways to reduce the costs enabling the aggressive pricing of the goods or services.

This is done by stripping all unnecessary peripheral features or services from the offering while simultaneously maintaining a focus on those product features which are indeed instrumental to how the customer perceives the performance of the product. Based upon the argument that the sustained development of peripheral services overshoots the expectations, or requirements, of how the majority of customers can utilize a discount strategy, a company seeks to compete on only those variables that hold significant value for the majority.

By reducing the number of peripheral services to those of essential value, the discount company will realize cost savings. These can be passed on to the customer allowing for an aggressive pricing of the product or service. In addition it will also create an increased focus on those parameters, which have been deemed important to the masses, allowing for an improved service in those areas.

Through such measures the discount strategy pursues a low cost strategy through the removal of all unnecessary peripheral services while simultaneously differentiating itself from the competition on the few variables essential to the customers' perception of the product and its performance.

When the two are combined effectively it creates a powerful vehicle for a company to truly differentiate itself from competitors as the traditional boundaries are broken. This is illustrated in Figure 3.2.

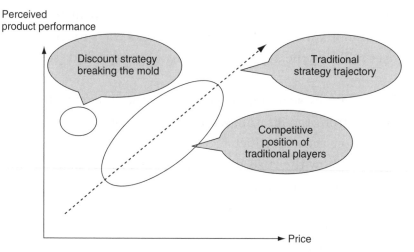

Figure 3.2 Discount strategy vs. traditional strategy

The removal of unnecessary peripheral services and product features may very well lead to a reduction in the perceived product performance. However, maintaining focus on key product features, such as on-time performance within the passenger airline industry, creates an improved relationship in terms of the price/quality ratio or at least the perception of such.

As can be seen from Figure 3.2, the discount strategy provides an opportunity to position a company outside the crowd of competitors who are pursuing one of the two traditional strategic paths to glory. In industries characterized by hyper-competition such a position will clearly send ripples through the water and signal to the customer that here is a company which offers something different . . . and perhaps even better.

How can a product or service be perceived as equal or superior if we have stripped it of all the advanced peripheral services and product features that everyone else is offering? Perhaps it is not better in the strictest sense of the word but it is perceived to offer a better value by those customers who have been overwhelmed by the sustained development of such peripherals and features. Such customers may wish for little more than the actual core product at a reasonable price.

When such a simplified product is offered at discount prices and it, furthermore, fares better than or equal to traditional products on specific key product or service features, a winner is born.

A single form – a simple form?

Is it really that simple then? Do you just strip your products or services to the core while maintaining a clear focus on what matters to the majority of customers and pass on the cost savings to those very customers?

Yes and no. The idea in itself may be simple but what is to be stripped from the product offering? What areas are of paramount importance to the customer as opposed to those that are just 'nice to have'? What kind of internal processes must be in place to support a discount strategy? How do you position such a product and the brand successfully in the market?

These questions may be answered by identifying the generic characteristics of successfully executed discount strategies, which is exactly what the following chapters aim to do through a detailed analysis and discussion of three companies operating in the discount mode.

The examples all represent some of the most successful applications of discount strategies and cover three diverse industries characterized by hyper-competition. The first of these case examples examines how a discount strategy was executed in one of the world's most competitive industries, namely the mobile telephony market.

4

CBB

Cultivating a hyper competitive market by way of a consistent approach to the notion of discount strategy

Right now, many in the mobile sector are struggling to find the right business models for the transition from the 2G market to the 3G market. At the same time, a new threat has emerged, the discount mobile service providers. We believe these discount mobile service providers will shake the market in a way not yet seen, even by the 3G/UMTS auctions.

John Strand, the Founder of Strand Consult

A contradiction to the bursting of the IT-bubble

Undoubtedly, adopting and implementing an adequate strategy seems especially important when dealing with hyper competitive environments.

Shortly after the IT-bubble burst, CBB Mobil [1] was established as a company in order to invent a new type of mobile telephony, namely pre-paid offerings marketed and delivered over the Internet. CBB Mobil went into para-commercial operation in May 2001 and failed catastrophically. However, during 2002 the company began implementing and adopting a discount strategy, which helped it to gain a certain foothold. By way of a more consistent approach to discount strategy, the company learned that not only was a sustainable foothold gained but a vibrant business was also to emerge quickly.

The story of CBB Mobil is therefore not only the story of the Ugly Duckling who initially suffered adversity and humiliation but in time turned into the most beautiful swan. The story of CBB Mobil is also the story of a company which exerted massive influence on its environment.

If you were hatched from a swan's egg, i.e. if you get the strategy right, a newcomer may outperform even in an established hyper competitive market.

The mobile sector – hyper-competition

CBB Mobil was established in the mobile communications sector in Denmark [2] in the latter half of the year 2000.

Originally, the mobile sector was characterized by a public utility monopoly. Gradually, competition was introduced, in the first place by way of a so-called second GSM operator,

1987:	Signature of the GSM Memorandum of Understand in Copenhagen
1991:	The issuing of the first licenses in Europe (in Germany and Denmark)
1992–1996:	Subsequent licensing of GSM1 and GSM2 operators in numerous other European countries, effectively creating *cosy duopolies*.
1996:	Licensing of third and fourth GSM operators, creating more competition
2000:	The UMTS auctioning of licenses, creating up to six national operators in many countries
2000:	Ample overcapacity in the networks leads to increasing focus on a more widespread opening-up for service providers and MVNOs
2005:	GSM MoU-organization counts more than 675 members based on network operations. In addition to network operators, service provision and MVNOs widely recognized in most European countries

Figure 4.1 GSM timeline

which established (cosy) duopolies during the first half of the 90's in Europe: see Figure 4.1.

During the second half of the 90's, more GSM licences were issued throughout Europe in order to increase competition. In the case of Denmark, two additional licences were issued in 1997, increasing the number of fully-fledged network-based operators to four in a country with around five million inhabitants. During 2001 this amount increased to five when the 3G licences were handed out and company '3' (owned by Hutchinson) subsequently entered the market.

By way of regulatory requirement, the network-based operators were obliged to open up their networks to service provision. Some nine service providers emerged who could, to some extent, benefit from the excess capacity of the network-based operators and thereby negotiate favorable prices.

This also happened to be the case at CBB who used a salami tactic in order to achieve gradual decreases in the wholesale prices obtained from Sonofon, one of the five operators.

However, the success of CBB was not due to a quick fix with regard to wholesale prices or any other single means of measurement. Over a period of 18 months, CBB managed to decrease the minute of usage charge from €0.23 to €0.09 whilst at the same time turning the company into comfortable profit.

The story to be told about CBB is the story of a company that started off by way of a Michael Porter based differentiator type of strategy but migrated successfully to the consistent development and implementation of a discount strategy. This migration did not only have a positive impact on CBB's own business case but also impacted on the commercial *modus operandi* of the entire mobile phone business.

What did the discount strategy contain and how was it successfully executed?

CBB as the enhanced service provider

Right from the beginning, CBB was established as a virtual provider, which means essentially that no network investments had to be made, as shown in Figure 4.2.

The underlying philosophy behind this was to exploit the excess network capacity in the existing five networks and the wholesale competition amongst the same.

Various types of service provision prevail in the mobile market ranging from pure resale to virtual network operations

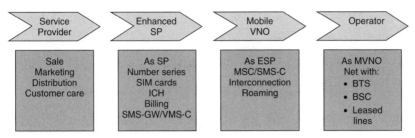

Figure 4.2 The value chain development from a service provider to an operator

(MVNO). Seen from the customers' point of view, CBB belonged to the latter end of the continuum, supported, *inter alia*, by the following characteristics:

- CBB established its own customer care system.

- A new billing system with Internet based payment transactions was established.

- The SIM-cards were branded proprietarily.

- A special CBB SIM tool kit menu was established with proprietary CBB services.

Consequently, the customers hardly noticed that CBB did not have their own network as all interaction with customers would stem from activities initiated or controlled by CBB.

The original mission and strategy

The company was incorporated on 5 December 2000 and went into semi-commercial operation on 21 May 2001.

Originally, the mission was to employ a prepaid business model internationally after a commercial launch in Denmark. The intention was not to become a price leader, but rather to follow a differentiator type of strategy.

On this basis, an Internet-based product was developed, including a content management system. This allowed the customer to conclude the entire sign up procedure on CBB's website. Once the customer had signed up, the customer gained access to a personal website from where the customer could top up and see the balance and itemization of the billing.

In terms of marketing strategy, CBB opted for a strong differentiation from the existing marketing players. With regard to branding, a community approach was taken by the adoption and marketing of 'Club Blah Blah', which was underpinned by the price structure, where a price reduction was given to calls within the 'Club Blah Blah' community.

Crisis and the filing of a petition for bankruptcy

During the commercial launch and the first year thereafter numerous problems arose which effectively put the company into a permanent state of crisis. Practically speaking, almost everything went wrong:

- Due to delays in the generation of billing data, customers' accounts were not updated in near real-time, which defeated the pre-paid concept and gave scope for fraud at an unacceptable level. Invariably, the customer care center had to constantly close and reopen customers' accounts manually.

- Such problems generated a permanent overload at the customer care center, which consequently was unable to provide customer service at an appropriate level.

- Numerous 'Club Blah Blah' advertisements were targeting youngsters who did not possess the necessary credit card facilities to top up their accounts electronically over the Internet.

- Towards the end of 2001, prices were cut in order to attract more customers but a satisfactory intake of customers was not achieved owing to the technical and marketing problems.

- In a last try, the company launched an off-line product branded Minutel. Due to continued technical problems, this further accelerated the crisis owing to immense problems with fraud.

During the summer of 2002, the owners of the company considered filing a petition for bankruptcy: the technology did not work, the billing procedures were inefficient, there was no money left for marketing, the debt level was exorbitant, and the number of active customers stood at around a mere 15,000.

However, instead of following this course of action, the owners decided to turn around the company by adopting and implementing a discount strategy. 'If you can't join them, beat them' seemed to be the competitive approach taken.

The discount strategy – not a single quick fix

The discount strategy embraced a complete renewal and change of the company. The contingencies for change were quite favorable as it was widely felt [3] that liquidation was a real threat.

New management

As a first step, a new CEO was recruited and a plan of action was agreed on prior to his taking on the assignment. During the recruitment process, the aim was to search for a profile that would develop the company quickly. This required IT leadership competence as well as a strong marketing background. The search process was concluded successfully after five months, and Teddy Søgaard Pedersen came on board as the new CEO during August 2002.

Teddy Søgaard Pedersen came equipped with more than 20 years' experience gained in executive positions at, amongst others, TDC, NSD and Telia Mobile. The combination of his past experience, his business development and IT skills and his personality was exactly what CBB needed to steer the company into profit. He soon began to appear in the media, raising the profile of CBB as the cheapest provider and

questioning both the establishment and certain business practices. One such example is his comment on the subject of
SIM locks.

> ... We do not interfere with the contractual obligations our
> customers may have with other companies. We just think that
> they should have the opportunity to use their mobile phone at
> the lowest prices in Denmark.

This comment was made on the back of a CBB campaign
offering to unlock the mobile phone of any new customer for
free if a start package was purchased.

Once the CEO seat had been occupied, internal operational
procedures came under scrutiny, starting with the IT-systems.

Reinvention of the IT-systems

The IT systems had to be reinvented. First of all, all transactions were moved to an IN-platform which allowed for a
debiting of the customers in real-time so that the customers
could see the balance in real-time, and so that the manual
opening up and closing down of accounts became superfluous.
Integration with the billing system was established, and the
capacity of the billing system was increased immensely.

A new website was established and appropriate steps were
taken to ensure that customers from then onwards were
able to get easy access to the site. The signing up procedure
was simplified and a comprehensive self-service program was
established.

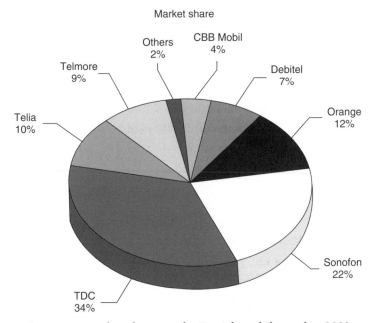

Figure 4.3 Market shares in the Danish mobile market 2003

In order to sustain this development, all IT functions were *insourced*, except for hosting. From the very beginning, all IT functions had been outsourced, but an assessment now showed later that not only was insourcing cheaper but also that speed with regard to how changes were implemented was improved.

All this was ready for the Christmas campaign of 2002, and the IT-systems were ready to elevate CBB's 0 % market share to 4 % market share during the following 12 months.

A new customer care concept

Under the differentiator strategy, CBB had invested modestly in customer care. Under the discount strategy these investments were increased considerably in order to lower the waiting time and to open up the customer care service during weekends.

Service level targets were set, and performance-related rewards agreed with the customer care team. Although the IT-systems and billing functioned smoothly, lowering the pressure from customers on these issues, even more staff and technological resources were dedicated to customer care.

As expected, the investment in customer care had a positive pay off and was well received by the customers. An independent end user study conducted by IDC in September 2003 showed that an amazing 96 % of respondents were satisfied with the services offered by CBB. In addition, consumer associations also ranked the customer care service favourably.

New brand and branding

Simultaneously, a complete re-branding process was launched. The 'Club Blah Blah' brand, which had mainly appealed to young people, was abandoned in order to increase the potential market. Thus, branding went hand in hand with a new segmentation where private customers in other age brackets and small and medium-sized enterprises were also addressed.

Moreover, the branding was renewed in numerous ways. By way of an example, advertisements for topping up at CBB were illustrated by a petrol pump with CBB's charges listed on the pump. The petrol pump, similar to the one shown in Figure 4.4, was also used in off-line advertisements in, e.g. retail shops.

Figure 4.4 The CBB petrol pump

The petrol pump was made deliberately futuristic looking in order not only to make a connection between filling up at a petrol station and topping up at CBB's website but also to represent a brand new way of doing things.

A marketing firm helped the management and the owners develop and implement a complete re-branding program. The right colours were carefully chosen in order to symbolize the discount values, the 'look and feel' of low price and high quality.

Reverse relationship marketing

Today, relationship marketing is widely accepted as conventional wisdom. It is also adopted by many mobile operators, which usually have a strong focus on subscription customers. Subscription allows the operator to build loyalty programs around each customer, e.g. by way of extra offerings at discounted rates, participation in competitions, instant communication, etc.

In the case of CBB, no loyalty programs were adopted. Customers could come and go as they pleased. The philosophy of discount in marketing was essentially that in order to retain customers, out of pocket expenses were wasted money. All the effort of CBB was therefore concentrated in making the core product as attractive as possible with regard to price and quality. No traditional peripheral services, such as loyalty programs, were offered.

Political mass marketing

As from the beginning of 2003, CBB introduced the media tactic of keeping the advertising budget low, whereas much energy was devoted to the feeding of journalists with interesting case stories. Positive information like the rapid intake of new customers, new services, increases in the quality of service level in the customer care functions, etc. received some attention and earned a few newspaper articles. Negative and/or aggressive news attracted considerable attention, such as conflict between CBB and its host operator, unfair treatment of CBB by its competitors, CBB challenging its competitors on price, etc.

CEO Teddy Søgaard Pedersen also fuelled the perception of CBB as the challenger through personal comments made to the media. On the subject of price he was quoted in September 2003:

> Our prices are more than 22 % lower than the nearest competitor. I am afraid to think of how much cheaper they are compared to many of the other expensive subscription packages that the large companies are offering.

Generally, journalists liked the idea of writing the story of CBB versus the incumbent (i.e. David and Goliath) as well as writing about CBB as a success. Part of the explanation for such popularity was that CBB positioned itself in strong contrast to, e.g. the incumbent, which was still remembered by customers as the (former) monopolist.

In terms of expenditure, this meant that CBB could operate at a very low level of marketing costs, in fact close to zero. The CBB brand was built not by costly advertising campaigns but primarily by journalists eager to tell the CBB story as that the ugly duckling that was fast becoming a white swan. This was galvanized by the fact that CBB managed to get onto prime time television at least five times during 2003.

Reorganization of the distribution

The formerly unsuccessful distribution was changed in several respects. First of all, the number of outlets was increased quickly to some 600 shops so that customers could sign up both over the Internet and through retail outlets.

Secondly, the off-line product itself was also changed. From viewing on-line and off-line as complementarily, the off-line product now came to be regarded as a first step to the on-line product, and customers were even told about the incentives to switch from an off-line solution to an on-line solution.

Last but not least, the logistics were completely changed. The distribution of SIM-cards was outsourced and the cost of producing SIM-cards and bringing them to the customers was lowered to one fifth of the former cost. The web-shop of terminal sales and accessories was also fully outsourced.

The comprehensive outsourcing of distribution stands in sharp contrast to the insourcing of all the IT-activities. The background for this 'dual' approach was that IT-competencies were defined as core competencies, whereas, e.g. physical distribution was defined as a non-core competence and not as critical to the mission of CBB.

Cost cutting programs

A detailed review of all cost items led to an unprecedented reduction of the level of costs. A few examples may illustrate how a true discount strategy was implemented.

Due to its very low marketing budget, CBB went to companies who had filed petitions for bankruptcy and got their prepaid advertisements in the newspapers and their spots on television virtually for free.

Another result of the consistent work-through of all cost items was that a Coca Cola machine from which the employees could buy drinks was removed, and instead CBB offered free soft drinks. Both CBB and the employees profited by this cost cut. CBB saved money and the employees now gained a true fringe benefit.

Active price leadership

An important cornerstone of the discount strategy was what could be labelled 'the role as the active price leader'.

Whenever competitors lowered their prices, CBB quickly followed suit, often within the same hour or so. Moreover, new services, such as MMS (multimedia messaging service) and GPRS (data communications) were priced very competitively.

As a result, CBB was perceived as the cost leader in the market.

CBB's discount product – cheaper and better

At the corporate level, all conceivable steps were taken to introduce and benefit from a discount strategy. But what does a mobile discount product look like? And what does discount mean?

Concerning the developed product, it had all the credentials associated with a standard mobile offering; the speech quality, the voice mail services, the SMS features and the data communications services were essentially the same in the market. The main differences were the innovative ways in which the product was produced and marketed.

Product production characteristics

As an Internet-based product, the customers can basically produce a considerable amount of the product themselves. They have access to a proprietary homepage where they can install their own service profile and where changes in their service profile can be made as desired, i.e. they do not need to contact a customer care center and fill in paper forms. In this way the customer is 'allowed' to be co-producer of the product, which increases the productivity and the efficiency for both CBB and for the customers. Customers often feel that they save time and that things work effectively when they are in control themselves.

As mentioned previously, the customers top up their accounts themselves. Based on a prepaid solution, the customer gains complete cost control and avoids a post-payable bill, as is the standard operating procedure under subscription terms and conditions. It is not possible for the customer to consume more than has been prepaid for because of the real-time feature where the customer's account is written down during the duration of a call on a per second basis and with a cut off if the customer has not topped up and the account balance reaches zero.

One of the implications of this is that CBB does not need to worry about bad debtors. The product is therefore open for everyone to join, where numerous other products in the market are restricted to customers with a credit worthy profile. Constraining certain groups in gaining access to certain services invariably creates public debate on discrimination against, e.g. persons with non-common names, living in certain areas, etc. CBB, however, was always able to market its product so that everybody was invited to join.

Concerning prices, the discount product is based on the principle of simplicity. Within the field of mobile communications, most national markets are characterized by four to six nationwide network operators and 10 service providers. Each provider has from five to 10 different price packages you can choose between and additional offerings promoted during campaigns, making up the total number of packages each customer is exposed to well above 100 at any point in time.

Against this background, CBB came out with just one, simple offering, namely no subscription fee and just one single minute of usage price applicable all day, for 24 hours, and charged on a per-second basis. Needless to say, the price of a discount product has to be very low or the lowest. In the case of CBB, the price was the lowest during much of the time and perceived to be the lowest for almost the rest of the time.

Furthermore, a discount product is characterized by a 'lean' structure, i.e. that all extras, value adds, volume discounts, special treatment of certain segments, 'if you buy this, you will obtain that', etc. are dispensed with. This is also the case with CBB's product, which was developed as a no-nonsense product. Bundling, which is one of the key characteristics of most products within the telecommunications sector, was left to the competitors. The CBB product is focused overwhelmingly on a single price of air time (voice telephony), and the only other charged services are services other than voice telephony, for which the competitors also charge, such as SMS, MMS, and GPRS. No bundling mechanisms prevail between voice telephony and the other services.

Conventional products are often constructed in such a way as to retain the customer. One of the predominant ways in the mobile sector is to supply subscription solutions which the customer cannot give up during a certain period and furthermore bundle such subscriptions with handset subsidies. The CBB product is not subjected to any such bounded financial irrationality. Rather, the CBB product is based on the loyalty the customers gain because of simplicity, consistent low price, and the cost control/self governance. With regard to handset subsidies, CBB stayed out of this business to the advantage of a very low air time price.

The customer care part of the CBB discount product is one of the most surprising. Many customers, and in particular CBB's competitors, would expect that a discount offering implied a poor customer service. As previously indicated, once CBB turned into a discount operator, the customer care service was improved immensely to the extent that the service surpassed the level of quality of many competitors. By labelling the CBB product a discount product, CBB had effectively lowered the customers' expectations of customer care considerably. However, actual performance as measured by low waiting time, long opening hours, friendly personnel, opportunities for self-service, etc. more than met the customers' level of expectation.

A last point of concern about the discount product was the criticism from competitors with regard to product development, namely that a discount product offering meant a farewell for the customers to advanced services or at least a late introduction to new services. This criticism withered away as it turned out that CBB's rate of product development was fairly good. CBB were among the first to introduce, e.g. MMS and GPRS services, and were the first on the market to introduce an enhanced proprietary voice mail service without a subscription fee. Later on, CBB also became the first company with a mobile messenger solution.

To sum up, CBB's discount product is cheap and, in many respects, better than those of the competitors, including customer care. The consumer associations concluded that 'not only is CBB (and Telmore, another discount provider) the cheapest, they also have the best customer care service' [4]. As is evident, the product differs considerably from the traditional products, and, importantly for a discount product, it is produced in an innovative, low cost way.

Product marketing characteristics

The development of a discount product turned out to be an almost sufficient criterion of success. Conventional wisdom states that advertisements and other promotional activities are the key to success. Without a good brand, even good products are practically worthless.

In the case of CBB, however, very limited marketing spending only turned out to be necessary for several reasons.

Firstly, the discount product is essentially an Internet based (e-trade) type of product. The main target group is people who use the Internet regularly and are confident with electronic payments. This means that a considerable amount of the marketing can take place through the Internet instead of, e.g. expensive whole-page advertisements in the daily newspapers. Internet marketing is, in many respects, free of charge. To take an example, many people frequent daily the discussion boards on the Internet. This means that an innovative product like CBB's product is discussed at length and such discussions are by definition costless and an excellent way of distributing knowledge about the product.

Secondly, the National Telecom Agency (IT- & Telestyrelsen) advertises price comparisons on the basis of an interactive price guide on the Internet hosted by the Agency as well as an off-line paper-based brochure which is distributed widely. CBB always compares favourably in such analyses and, for a long time, they were ranked as the cheapest provider. The price comparisons have been quoted regularly in the newspapers and in the telecom journals. Consequently, many customers sign up solely on the basis of such comparisons gained at no marketing expenditure.

Moreover, CBB has found creative ways of getting onto the prime time television news and into the newspapers with advertisements at no marketing expenditure or – when it was necessary to pay for promotional activities – to do this diligently and at a much lower cost than that of its competitors [5].

Lastly, it turned out that discount customers are much more customer acquisition focused than subscription customers. Discount customers generally liked the idea of acting as ambassadors for the discount company, and CBB sustained this trend with a 'member-get-member-bonus'.

In summary, it is probably easier to market a well-functioning discount product than a conventional product as self-selling mechanisms can be exploited and as the normal very costly built-up of a brand can be mitigated significantly with a discount strategy. One of the obvious reasons will be outlined in the following section, namely the attention and attraction that a company or a product receives when participating in price wars.

CBB's use of price as a tactical weapon

Obviously, one of the building blocks of a discount strategy is to use price as a tactical weapon. This does not only involve the price level but also the marketing of the price as well as price expectations. In a hyper competitive market it is furthermore a necessary condition to be able to match the reactions of the competitors in order to be able to control the contingencies of price wars.

The importance of the price vis-à-vis the customers

In a hyper competitive market where the basic part of the product, in this case plain old mobile voice telephony, is practically the same, price inevitably becomes an important driver in penetration of new segments. In addition, price is also an important vehicle for capturing customers from the competition and by this increasing the churn of the competitors' customers.

Through sustained marketing on price, both existing and potentially new customers gain confidence in a company, which often generates expressions like: 'I think that they will continue to stay as the cheapest company' or 'I trust them because I can count on them lowering the price'. An active (perceived) price leadership, therefore, both generates retention of existing customers and demand pull from new customers.

Invariably, both the positive retention and the demand pull effect help keeping the acquisition cost at a very low level.

Active leadership in price wars

CBB has consistently stayed away from demanding a subscription fee from customers. This turned out to be an important and unique selling proposition, because the main focus of the existing operators had been to shift customers from prepaid solutions to subscription packages. Moreover, the existing operators, from time to time, tried to increase the subscription charge in return for a cheaper minute of usage price. However, fixed price increases are generally not well received by customers in a hyper competitive market. 'What do I get for my subscription fee and where does the money go?' is a common customer complaint.

With no subscription fee, much attention was attracted to the minute of usage price. Originally, CBB started off with DKK 1.75 (€ 0.23) and lowered this price to DKK 1.10 (€ 0.15), which was then clearly the cheapest offering. However, when a competitor (Telmore, bought by the incumbent) lowered its price to DKK 1.10 (€ 0.15), CBB went under DKK 1 (€ 0.13) with a DKK 0.99 offering on April 1, 2003.

Sinking below DKK 1 turned out to be an important price point because the effect was immense coverage in the press, talking about 'CBB breaking the wall' and 'an unprecedented low price'. For a long time, CBB remained in the position of having the lowest price of all, and CBB's courageous price move meant that it took the role of the active price leader in the market.

During the second half of 2003, CBB's price was further cut to DKK 0.85 (€ 0.11), DKK 0.74, and DKK 0.69 (€ 0.09), all inclusive of the applicable 25 % VAT. At this time, however, it is remarkable that the price decreases were not initiated by CBB but were reactions to price decreases from competitors. The development in prices charged by individual companies is shown in Figure 4.5 [6]

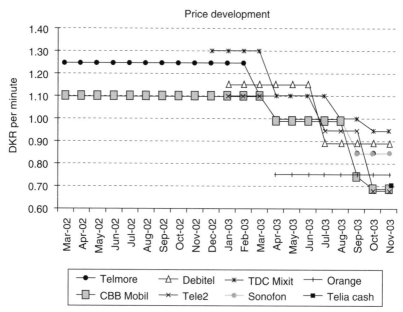

Figure 4.5 The rapid price decline in the minutes of usage charges during 2003

Three points with regard to CBB's role in the price war during the second half of 2003 need to be elaborated. Firstly, CBB's reaction as a price decrease follower came rather quickly, in some cases within a couple of hours, so that the media and customers might have found it difficult to work out who was the leader and who was the follower. Secondly, CBB continued to take the position of having the cheapest price, which also seemed to be indisputable as against any follower syndrome.

A third point is that CBB's CEO, Teddy Søgaard Pedersen, stated consistently in press releases and comments to the public that 'The price war is not over yet. We shall soon see prices as low as DKK 0.50'. From time to time the CEO even stated that the prices would shrink 'below DKK 0.50'. This also helped facilitate the active role of CBB in the price wars.

In areas other than the minute of usage price, CBB's aggressive price policy was evident. As an example, all the other providers had set the price of an MMS at DKK 3 (€0.40). CBB suddenly lowered its price to DKK 1.99 (€0.27). In addition, CBB entered into a marketing campaign by way of press releases and announcements to the press (again, no marketing expenditure was incurred) claiming that the other providers had formed a hidden cartel to make the price of an MMS stay at the high level of DKK 3. Not surprisingly, the headline of the CBB campaign was 'CBB is now breaking the price cartel on MMS.'

By deliberately using prices as a tactical weapon, CBB obtained a market position as the (perceived) price leader, which is highly consistent with a discount strategy.

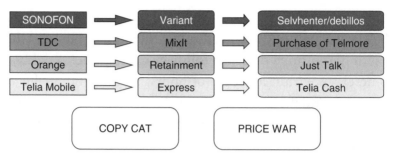

Figure 4.6 Incumbents' and established players' copycatting discount strategies

A further consolidation of this tactic was evident when, during 2003, all the network operators tried to copy of the discount concept, as illustrated in Figure 4.6.

The fact that the 'old' competitors had to copy the CBB concept indicated to the entire market that the customer got a good deal with a discount provider like CBB.

Results – best in class

Was the turn around of CBB by way of a discount strategy effective in financial terms? Is it likely that an alternative strategy could have generated better financial results?

Seen from a cash flow perspective, the strategy so far seems to be attractive. During the start-up of the company and during times when the crisis in the telecom sector made the cash flow of many companies the most important issue on the agenda, CBB was never cash-strapped. This stems from the fact that all customers are required to make pre-payments, whereas CBB makes post-payments to its suppliers, notably the host operator. On average, CBB has the opportunity of post-paying at least 45 days after the consumption has taken place.

The profit and loss accounts speak for themselves, starting off with a deficit of DKK 11 million (€1.5 million) in 2001, which was turned into profits of DKK 10 million (€1.33 million) in 2002 and DKK 20 million (€2.7 million) in 2003. At the same time, the customer base grew from around 15,000 customers, when the discount strategy was adopted in the autumn of 2002, to close to 200,000 customers when the shares of the company were sold off in the Spring of 2004 [7].

How does this compare with the other players in the market?

Figure 4.7 provides some guidance with respect to a consolidated answer.

It is remarkable that only TDC earns profits among the existing 'old' operators. Telia and Orange lose around DKK 1,000 (€133) per year per customer. However, the discount providers earn money, and, as can be seen, CBB earns the most per customer, around DKK 139 (€19) yearly per customer.

Profit before tax per customer during 2003			
Discount companies		**The 'old' companies**	
CBB	139 DKK (€19)	Sonofon	0 DKK (€0)
Telmore	71 DKK (€9)	Orange (estimated)	−880 DKK (−€117)
		Telia (estimated)	−1,000 DKK (−€133)
		TDC	550 DKK (€73)

Figure 4.7 Profit and loss examples

Analyses have shown that considerable cost-based ineffi-
ciencies prevail among the existing operators [8], who have
not implemented a consistent discount strategy, but have
launched competing discount products.

The case history of CBB is not just a story of the discount
product but more a story about the consistent implementation
of a comprehensive discount strategy.

A revolution in the mobile sector?

Nobody knows where the saturation of the discount market
lies. However, on average, TDC and Sonofon effectively
charge their customers slightly above DKK 2 (€0.27) per
minute [9], whereas CBB charges DKK 0.69 (€0.09) per minute.

All the existing operators and some of the new entrants have
introduced discount offerings in order to copy the offerings
from CBB and to some extent, Telmore. So far, most of the
attention has been focused on private customers, but towards
the beginning of 2004, CBB began to take up a relatively high
number of business customers, in particular among small and
medium-sized enterprises and in accordance with its segmentation policy, as displayed in Figure 4.8.

Both the demonstrable success in the private sector and the
quick take up of customers in the business sector imply that
the general price level for voice minutes will decline gradually
from the industry average of the existing players of around
DKK 2 (€0.3) per minute to a price of DKK 0.69 (€0.09).

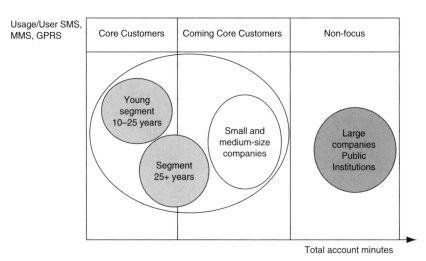

Figure 4.8 Segmentation in a discount mobile strategy

Whether the incumbent market leader today (TDC) can retain its long-term profitability will probably have less to do with the introduction and charging of the new services than with whether they can adapt quickly to the cost structure of a discount provider. Concerning Telia, Orange, and, to a very limited extent, Sonofon, the starting point were deficits. Under the prevailing price regime, the situation now requires them to make accurate and very far-reaching decisions on the implementation of discount principles in order to even reach true break-even.

The incumbent bought Telmore out of the market at the beginning of 2003 and a year later Sonofon bought shares in CBB. One can therefore ask whether it is possible to buy the discount providers out of the market and afterwards enjoy a cartel-like cosiness without price competition. However, this is not realistic owing to several factors. One is that some of the new carbon copy discount providers have launched low prices, such as Tele2, who markets an almost similar type of discount product priced at DKK 0.68 (€ 0.09). Another is that 3 has launched a package where not only a discount price of DKK 0.69 (€ 0.09) is heavily promoted but also 3 internal network calls are entirely free of charge. Thus, it is not as if the existing operators can get away with a price increase, given the rivalry in the market.

Not surprisingly, a number of other markets among the European countries fear the introduction of CBB-like discount products and strategies, labelled the 'Danish disease'.

Perspectives

Nobody knows what the future will bring. However based upon our past and present experience, we may draw the following conclusions:

- CBB and others have ably demonstrated in the mobile sector that e-trade is a commercial reality far beyond the expectations of industry analysts.

- The crisis at CBB was exploited constructively in order to achieve a turn around of the company on the basis of a discount strategy.

- Developing a discount product diligently is an obvious candidate of choice benchmarked against the existing 'more of the same' relationship marketing approach.

- Some kind of active price leadership needs to go hand in hand with cost cutting programs in order to achieve profitability.

- From a corporate point of view, the early adoption and implementation of a discount strategy, in an almost saturated market, provides a considerable amount of exposure as the media are often keen on innovative projects. And this is even more so if some of the offerings and changes come suddenly.

- Once a provider succeeds in pulling a consistent discount strategy together, the market, including competitors, has no 'return ticket', and an irreversible process has been initiated.

The story of CBB and its fellow discount providers is therefore, above all, the story of a new industry strategy which – once introduced – will make it impossible for the market participants to revert to square one. The discount providers can cultivate a hyper competitive market if the strategy is developed and implemented consistently. It did not take CBB much more than a year to gain a 4 % market share of a saturated market, to cut the prices to almost one third, and to become the most profitable among 13 competitors, surpassed with regard to profitability only by the incumbent, which had enjoyed a monopoly and which, furthermore, enjoys economies of scale and scope.

However, the 'old' operators, including the incumbent, all appear to have been caught by surprise and to face a Gordian Knot which cannot be untied: on the one hand, they have to join the discount offerings in order to retain customers and to still have a chance to take up new customers. On the other, they face numerous problems when they follow suit, e.g. an exorbitant loss of revenue because the existing customers move effectively from €0.27 to around €0.09 per minute and because it is almost 'mission impossible' for the incumbent to switch to production costs at the level of an efficient discount provider.

5
Lidl

Gaining ground in a hyper competitive market by a consistent discount strategy

There is nothing little about Lidl

Alex Biesada, Hoovers online

The German conquest

Continuous implementation of the right strategy is of paramount importance in an environment of immense competition.

With a history in fruit and vegetable wholesale and cash & carry, Lidl established their first grocery retail store in Germany in 1973. Initially, Lidl copied Aldi closely by offering customers a limited range of products at a low price [1]. This was developed further and Lidl established their own profile resulting in larger stores and a greater range than

Aldi. By implementing and focusing on a discount strategy consistently, Lidl established itself in the German market and gained a position from which they could take on larger competitors. Over the following three decades, Lidl grew into a European player and one which was feared by its competitors.

The story of Lidl is therefore not just that of a German phenomenon but the story of how their focus on discount gave them a European presence and a feared reputation across Europe.

The grocery retail sector – hyper-competition

The competitive nature of the grocery retail sector has traditionally taken the form of national oligopolies characterized by a few large and many smaller players. The actual store concept has developed since the first self-service store was established in the 50's with the introduction of supermarkets and hypermarkets during the 60's, the introduction of discount stores in the 70's, and lastly convenience stores which emerged in the 80's. The difference between these four store concepts is mainly in terms of the amount and nature of articles stocked, in-store equipment, and the size of the actual store. A discount store typically holds 800–1,000 articles compared to 7,000–9,000 held by hypermarkets, with the supermarket holding slightly less than that of a hypermarket. Figure 5.1 provides a timeline view of this development.

Grocery Retail development

1950–1979	1980	1990	2000	2004
Self service stores	Cassis de Dijon (1979)	European Discount growth	Discount threat	Discount Leading
Self service is introduced in the early 1950's	Rewe applied to the German spirits monopoly for permission to import 'Cassis de Dijon' – denied due to a low alcohol percentage	From 1991 to 1999 the market share of Discount grows from 9.4% to 15.0%	Further growth planned by Lidl to include the Nordics, Baltics and the East	In 2003, Aldi and the Schwarz Group are placed as the 6th and 7th largest Grocery retailer in Europe
First Hypermarket opens in 1963	The case goes to the European Court of Justice on the issue of whether a member state can legally impose minimum alcohol content rules	During the same period, Lidl grows their number of stores from 754 to 3441. New stores in Italy, Spain, UK, Belgium, Portugal, NL, Austria and Greece	Lidl opens an additional 1000 stores in the first three years of the new millenium	
On the back of the oil crisis in the early 1970's, Discount stores are gaining ground in particularly Germany	ECJ rules that in principle each member state must give access to goods accepted as fit for sale in another EU Market			

Figure 5.1 Grocery retail timeline

These four different concepts were up until the mid-80's established within national borders and the competitive situation was therefore characterized by national oligopolies. Supermarkets and hypermarkets had established themselves as the dominant concept of grocery retailing across Western Europe when the discount concept was introduced in the early 70's driven by the idea that roughly 20 % of store items typically account for nearly 80 % of the turnover. The discount store aims to hold those items with a high inventory turnover and reduce the price of these by lowering costs, stemming from having a larger mix of goods. The supermarkets and hypermarkets countered this new concept by increasing the number of fresh foods and adding non-food items to their mix of articles under the strategy of one-stop-shopping.

The discount concept has traditionally been considered a German phenomenon with Aldi and Lidl as the two large discount chains dominating the German market. This perception has changed since the mid-80's given the rapid international expansion of these two and also the emergence of other players pursuing a similar strategy.

The European nature of the grocery retail sector was sparked by the 1979 European Court of Justice ruling in the famous 'Cassis de Dijon' case, which was brought to the attention of the EU by REWE, a German based cooperative. The case concerned the import of the French liqueur 'Cassis de Dijon' for sale to the German market, which the German spirits monopoly blocked initially on the grounds of the alcohol percentage being too low. The Court's ruling went against this initial prohibition and stated that any product accepted as fit for sale in one EU member state could be sold in another EU member state as this was the basic concept behind the free movement of goods. Grocery retail could therefore make the jump from being a mainly domestic to a European business with any EU retailer having the right to expand into any other EU member state with its current product assortment, leaving the choice of store and choice of products entirely up to the consumer and his or her preferences.

Despite this ruling in 1979, many of today's major players did not expand significantly until the late 80's when one can argue that the European grocery retail market was born. A true European market for grocery retail was, however, first established when the US based WalMart, the world's largest grocery retail chain, entered the European continent. Striking fear into the players already operating in Europe, the entrance of WalMart initiated a spree of consolidation in the industry and Co-ops began to appear.

Today a significant amount of sales for the top players originate from outside their domestic market. Figure 5.2 shows the percentage of sales outside the country of origin for some of the major players, indicating the size of European operation [2].

The concepts of supermarket and hypermarket are represented here by Carrefour, Auchan and Tesco whereas Aldi and Lidl

Company	Origin	First EU expansion	Net Sales 2004	Domestic sales 2004	Foreign sales 2004
Carrefour	France	1973, Spain	€ 72.688 Mio	49.1 %	50.9 %
MetroGroup	Germany	Unknown	€ 56.409 Mio	52.3 %	47.7 %
Tesco	UK	Unknown	€ 50.092 Mio	79.3 %	20.7 %
Auchan	France	1981, Spain	€ 35.978 Mio	54.4 %	45.6 %
Lidl (Schwarz)	Germany	1989, France	€ 34.263 Mio	58.2 %	41.8 %
Aldi	Germany	Unknown	€ 33.708 Mio	59.6 %	40.4

Figure 5.2 Domestic and foreign sales of major European players

represent the discount concept and the Metro group covers cash and carry, food retail and specialist stores.

The nature of the European market for grocery retail can be argued to consist of all these various formats, thus laying the traditional view of the discount store as a German phenomenon firmly to rest. This is further emphasized by the growth in discount market share estimated by Retail Institute Scandinavia [3] as shown in Figure 5.3.

Over the past two decades the market for grocery retail has broken down the borders that previously existed between countries resulting in a European arena where it is no longer the supermarkets and hypermarkets that enjoy unrivalled existence. The discount stores have entered this arena, claiming their share of the market. Lidl started their operations based on the model used by Aldi but have since added to their assortment and created their own unique profile in Europe.

However, the success of Lidl is more than a tale of selling lower quality at lower prices. It is a story of a company which, through a focused discount strategy, has enjoyed not only tremendous growth but has also managed to shape the

Country	Discount market share 2003	Expected discount market share 2014
Germany	40%	60%
France	10%	20%
Denmark	28%	45%
Sweden	10%	20%
Norway	46%	50%

Figure 5.3 Discount market shares in selected European countries

industry in which they are now among the top 10 European performers.

What does this discount strategy consist of and how has Lidl successfully managed to implement and execute this strategy?

The original mission and strategy of Lidl

The Schwarz Group emerged in 1930 when Josef Schwarz became a partner in Sudfruchte Grosshandel Lidl & Co, which at that time was a fruit wholesaler. Josef Schwarz then transformed the company into a general food wholesaler, renaming it Lidl & Schwarz. When his son, Dieter Schwarz, took over the company it began to focus on discount markets, larger supermarkets and cash and carry wholesale markets. One initial problem Dieter Schwarz was faced with was that he didn't have the rights to use the name of Lidl, and 'Schwarz Markt', meaning 'Black Market', didn't seem such a good idea. However, he purchased the right to use the name from a retired teacher by the name of Ludwig Lidl for a thousand German marks and Lidl became a reality. Since the first store was opened in 1973 Lidl has enjoyed considerable success and is now considered to be the foundation of the success of the Schwarz Group.

The first Lidl stores were developed by copying the Aldi concept as closely as possible. This focused on selling articles with a high average turnover in the stores and making these available at low prices through effective operations and a low

Figure 5.4 The original business model

level of service [4]. The original business model is in fact fairly simple and can be depicted as shown in Figure 5.4.

However, in time Lidl developed this concept further by adding more articles to their assortment and through new innovative approaches. Given this they managed to create their own unique profile among the customers under the philosophy

The Best Quality at the Lowest Prices

This business model clearly demands a strong focus on costs but there is more to a successful discount strategy. Simplicity across all areas of business is put forward by Lidl as one of the key parameters for their success.

The discount strategy – all encompassing

Over the past three decades Lidl has managed to grow into one of the most significant discount retailers on the European continent with a presence in Italy, Spain, France, UK, Belgium, Portugal, Holland, Austria and Greece as well as in Eastern Europe and Scandinavia. This has been achieved by a strong focus on not just a single variable but through a number of factors leading to the discount strategy being all encompassing.

Structured to control the impact of external factors

Lidl is part of the Schwarz Group owned mainly by Dieter Schwarz through the Dieter Schwarz Stiftung, which owns 99.9 % of the holding company, Schwarz Beteiligungs GmbH, the group's holding company [5].

The Schwarz Group consists of Lidl, 'Kaufland', 'Handelshof' and 'Concord' which are hyper- and supermarkets, 'Ruef' which is a wholesale market and 'Warenhandels GmbH' and 'Lidl Discount', which are both purchasing units. These are all organized under the two main divisions of the Schwarz Group, the Kaufland Stiftung & Co. KG and Lidl Stiftung & Co. KG.

The structure of Lidl Stiftung & Co. KG and the Lidl stores is comprised of 400 to 500 minor companies. This minimizes the obligation to give information and as such the dissemination of any financial or strategic information. Furthermore, the smaller size of these individual companies reduces intervention from trade unions, work councils and shop stewards, allowing Lidl to negotiate compensation packages directly with their employees. Very little is in fact known externally about what goes on behind the scenes at Lidl and hence an aura of mystery surrounds the company.

Dieter Schwarz has clearly been instrumental in developing the secrecy which surrounds Lidl to the point that it even surpasses that of Aldi. As a person he is equally reluctant to appear in the media and to give interviews, which has led some journalists to argue that he is harder to find than the yeti.

Leadership through continuity

The man behind Lidl, Dieter Schwarz, has gained a mythical status in Germany through his aversion to publicity, which has gained Lidl tremendous exposure in the media. He has throughout the past three decades steered Lidl towards becoming one of the largest grocery retailers in Europe. This continuity in having the same top executive is assumed to be one key reason for their success in that every member of the organization has been clear on the path he or she was taking and be confident that there would be no immediate changes to the strategy or decisions made [6].

Having handed the management of Lidl to Klaus Gehrig, the spokesman for the board, the company is still kept under a tight rein with centralized management and disclosure of just as little information as before.

The look and feel of Lidl

The format of a discount store is organized in a very different manner from that of a traditional supermarket. Not only does the discount store hold a very limited number of goods but their presentation is also different. The goods are presented in bulk, meaning that they are often displayed while still on the pallet, as shown in Figure 5.5, thus lowering the cost of display and the number of staff needed.

Figure 5.5 Inside Lidl

This, as well as the easy access around the store increases the speed at which articles can be delivered from stock to store while creating a sense of well organized simplicity for the customer.

The location of the store itself is another area where Lidl is different from many traditional supermarkets given that Lidl seems to place their stores away from the city centers with easy access and lower rent. All Lidl stores are constructed in a simple manner, adding to the simplicity of the store. Simplicity is a key variable for Lidl as they seek to simplify all operations and pass on cost savings to the consumers.

Lidl has had an historical focus on grocery items but has begun to add non-food items to their assortment such as bicycles, clothes, shoes, consumer electronics and PCs. Such non-food items are displayed in the center of the store in order to guide the consumer when hunting for seasonal offers pertaining to these non-food items. An example of this type of lay-out is shown in Figure 5.6. [7]

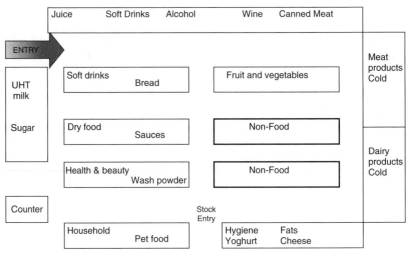

Figure 5.6 Store outline

The addition of non-food items is clearly outside the normal scope of a true discount store but both Lidl and Aldi have managed to introduce such items successfully through seasonal offerings.

The simplicity of this store lay-out allows the customers to become oriented quickly as to the placement of goods they seek. It also promotes efficiency as the customers will need a very limited amount of assistance in finding what they seek. This has lead to a superior performance in average sales per square meter of floor space for Lidl when compared to that of a traditional supermarket [8]. According to a McKinsey survey, Lidl has sales of € 5.400 per square meter whereas the traditional supermarket displayed average sales of € 3.900 per square meter.

The efficiency with which Lidl manages to create a high turnover of goods is aided by their simple store layout and low number of articles held and provides them with a key advantage over their traditional rivals.

Efficiency, however, is not enough to sustain a successful business model within the grocery retail sector unless the customer perceives the product or store as one of good value.

High service level with a discount concept

The customer service concept is driven primarily by price and simplicity in order to underline the philosophy of Lidl which is 'The best quality at the lowest prices'.

However, other areas such as the opportunity to pay with EC cards (Electronic Cash), little waiting time at the counter, in store service, and perhaps somewhat surprisingly, the freshness of their products are put forward by Lidl as parameters for increased customer service.

A question of greater interest is, however, how the customer actually perceives the service and what factors are of influence when selecting a store. From a brand-health survey conducted by McKinsey in Germany in 2003 where 750 German shoppers were interviewed, the two discount chains Lidl and Aldi actually fared better on variables believed to be the stronghold of their traditional German rivals REWE and Edeka, which the illustration in Figure 5.7 highlights [9].

Convenience, innovation and affinity, in particular, are areas where the discount stores score higher but the close race on assortment and service where traditional stores should hold an advantage is perhaps more remarkable.

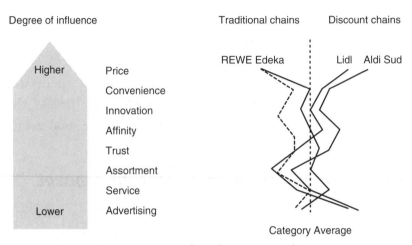

Figure 5.7 Criteria for selecting a retail store

The data in the figure above are based on Aldi Sud and Lidl Germany only, and should as such not be seen as representative of all of their operations Europe wide. However, the interesting points regarding what customers perceive to be of value and how these two discount chains fare, compared to traditional supermarkets, are argued to be of a generic nature.

One reason for this is the emergence of the 'discount generation' [10]. This generation of consumers, born predominantly in the 70's and 80's, has been exposed to the discount phenomenon throughout their lives and have grown accustomed to doing their shopping in this type of store. This is said to be similar to the feelings of the 'supermarket generation', who were born in the 40's and 50's for whom the supermarkets were the natural choice of shopping.

This shift in shopping patterns among customers is accompanied by a blurring of the borders between what constitutes a supermarket and a discount store. According to Retail

Institute Scandinavia, this is shown by the large number of consumers that perceive certain discount stores as supermarkets. An example of this is that out of 225 female respondents aged between 28 and 36, 28 % gave the name of a discount store when asked to name their favourite supermarket [11].

This acceptance of discount stores among customers has aided Lidl in their campaign for market share and the fact that they are perceived as providing equal service and nearly the same assortment but at a substantially lower price is another key to their success. One of the reasons they manage to do so can be attributed to the large number of private labels, which is discussed in the following section.

Squeezing the brands

In terms of the products supplied and thus found on the shelves of a Lidl store, a vast majority are characterized by being private label products. A private label product is a product produced for the individual retailer as opposed to brand names such as 'Pampers diapers'. Such products are assumed to create a price reduction in the region of 10 to 20 % thus providing the retailer with the opportunity to pass these savings on to the customers [12].

The assortment found in a Lidl store consists of 85 % private labels providing them with the opportunity to not only sell the products at a lower price but also allowing for some form of uniqueness. Lidl has used this method to position their products not in terms of higher quality, thus a higher price, but equal quality at a lower price.

This is underlined by the fact that 85 % of the respondents in a 'Shopper study' conducted by AC Nielsen agreed with the following statement:

The discounters offer the same quality as super- and hypermarkets.

One reason for this is the quality control measures that Lidl has put into place to ensure the high quality of their private label products [13].

An example of the less fortunate impact that the private labels can have is the online article published on subvulture.com, a satirical humour website, where two of Lidl's beverage products are given a satirical salute. The products in question are an energy drink and a beer, as shown in Figure 5.8.

On occasion a product is discovered so special that it merits its own attempt at copyright infringement. This is the case with 'Sitting Bull energy drink', maintaining the 'Bull' in its own right and inferring the 'Red' with cunning use of a Red Indian motif. Close as it was, the sitting part of the name detracted from the overall impression of energy more than was retained by the rest of the packaging. Perhaps this mixed success was due to a splitting of marketing funds with 'Seriously Draught Bitter'. Although its canned status clearly denotes that it is not draught, I feel that 'Seriously' is sufficiently convincing for this product to succeed.

http://www.subvulture.com/archive/022.html, Author unknown

Despite concerns regarding the labelling of products and whether it is incomplete there is little doubt that Lidl's private

Figure 5.8 Examples of labelling

label strategy is another key to their immense success. This, paired with a reputation for being hard negotiators when approaching their suppliers has resulted in a situation where they can offer similar or equal quality at lower prices.

Aggressive go to market strategy

The name 'Lidl' has been a well known name among German consumers for decades given their blatant copying of the Aldi concept and the fierce price wars these two discount chains have engaged in over the years. However, they do not yet enjoy an equal recognition outside of Germany where the discount phenomenon has been attributed to local players. Through a very aggressive 'go-to market' strategy when expanding in Europe, Lidl is seeking to remedy this. This strategy is, in all its simplicity, characterized by opening a large number of stores in a short span of time. The average number of stores opened per year for the last 10 years is 301 compared to, e.g. Aldi's 216.

From 1991 to 2002 they increased their number of stores from 754 to 4,429 and from being established in Germany and France alone to a presence in 13 countries.

When comparing this growth to other discount stores it becomes evident that Lidl is expanding its presence across Europe at a higher pace than other discount operators: see Figure 5.9 [14].

All Lidl stores are similar in their look and feel with simplicity as the main characteristic. Everything from their blue and yellow logo with the red 'l' in italics situated above the entrance of the simple building to the functional layout of the store signals simplicity. This is a mantra they also use to promote through their online universe (www.lidl.fr) and advertising campaigns, which highlights the uncompli-cated nature of their underlying philosophy as well as the customer's experience when shopping at Lidl. This, paired with the perception of Lidl as one of the cheapest grocery retail chains, adds up to a powerful brand, feared by the majority of

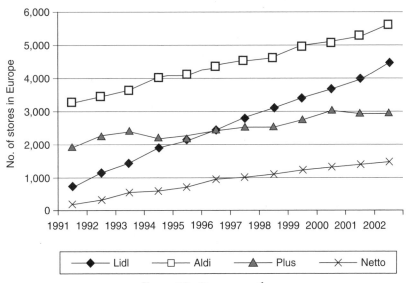

Figure 5.9 Store growth

competitors both in markets where they are currently operating and those they have disclosed as possible for expansion.

As mentioned previously, the traditional view of a discount store as a place many consumers would rather not be seen in has eroded over the past decade. This may be the result of the strong branding process of the largest operators and their skill in convincing consumers that they do indeed offer the best value for money. It may also have been accelerated by the recent economic downturn. However, there is no doubt that the discount store as a concept has gained a foothold beyond the German borders and that Lidl as a discount chain is looking to build its brand into a European context.

The impact of the Lidl name outside the German borders is astonishing when considering that very little information is leaked to the public about future plans. One would almost argue that the mere possibility of Lidl entering a market stirs the waters in such a way that marketing, including the usual brand awareness building campaigns, becomes unnecessary for Lidl. This one could attribute to the brand they have managed to build with such secrecy over the past three decades.

Publicity through secrecy

The secret nature of operations championed by founder Dieter Schwarz and maintained throughout the history of Lidl has earned the chain a considerable amount of press coverage. An example of this is that no less than 2,493 hits are shown on Norwegian net based newspapers since January 2002 when performing a search on Kvasir's newsagent [15]. Speculation as to whether secrecy is indeed part of Lidl's media strategy has therefore grown, adding to the publicity that Lidl gains.

The battle with Aldi for the position as the leading discount store has also generated media attention. This is especially the case in Germany where this battle has been personified by the founders of Aldi, Theo and Karl Albrecht in one corner and Dieter Schwarz in the other.

Such political mass marketing has most certainly enhanced the perception among the public of Lidl as a discount chain which not only offers low-priced products but also manages to exert pressure on the prices charged by other grocery retailers. A survey conducted in Finland by AC Nielsen shows that immediately after the opening of the first Finnish Lidl store the price level dropped by 1.6 % over the period of July to September.

On a less flattering note, Lidl's secretiveness has also generated publicity concerning the incomplete labelling of their private label products, product safety and food cleanliness. Despite this there is little doubt that the publicity generated and the immediate reaction from competitors aid Lidl in creating a perception among customers that they are indeed the chain offering products at the lowest prices.

Active price leadership

Considering the underlying philosophy of Lidl which aims to offer the 'Best quality at the lowest price', the perception among customers of Lidl being the price leader is of considerable importance. It is hard to ascertain whether they are indeed offering the goods at the lowest price but the perception of Lidl among customers is that they are a price leader.

This is achieved by targeting groups of items which they 'attack' when entering a new market and through seasonal offerings. Examples of such entry products are beer, juice, soft drinks and confectionary. In addition to this they use consumer surveys to illustrate their position as the price leader. However, on at least one occasion, this tactic has earned them a slap on the wrist from a Spanish consumer organization which was misquoted in a Lidl advert as proclaiming that Lidl offered the lowest prices.

Despite this, the goods offered by Lidl and their prices have attracted many consumers across Europe, and the question which remains to be answered is whether these products can indeed be argued to offer equal quality at lower prices?

Lidl's discount product – cheaper and better

Lidl's product is more than just one product. It is the assortment carried in the stores, the accessibility of the stores, the simplicity of their layout, and the experience the customers gain from shopping there. As such, one cannot isolate one particular product when assessing whether the product offered by Lidl is indeed cheaper and better. A number of factors must be viewed in order to assess this.

The first factor pertains to the assortment carried in the store. In other words what do they sell? As mentioned earlier, the underlying philosophy of a discount store is to carry groceries with a high turnover, meaning those articles used frequently in a household. These are also argued to be the basic goods used in a household and are estimated to account for nearly 80 % of a household's grocery expenditure [16]. As simple as this may sound, these articles must, however, match the customers' needs and the changes in these needs. Lidl carries an assortment of roughly 1,000 articles in its stores and has gained a reputation for responding to changing customer needs more swiftly than, i.e. their main competitor Aldi. An example of such a change in behavior is the increase in purchases of frozen foods, which has generally been seen over the past two decades and the increase in assortment that such a shift in customer needs necessitates.

When comparing the average shopping basket at Lidl to that of all shopping baskets, as displayed in Figure 5.10, it is evident

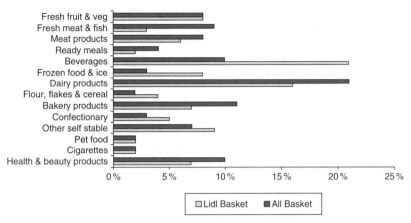

Figure 5.10 Average shopping basket

that they do hold the same range of articles, although offering a reduced variety within each category [17].

Given this, the range held by Lidl does mirror that of a traditional supermarket in terms of different product categories and more importantly, it satisfies the majority of needs displayed by the grocery customers. A few of the key categories for Lidl are: beverages, frozen food and ice cream, and flour, flakes and cereal, which one would expect. However, the percentage of fresh fruit and vegetables indicates that they have managed to add to their assortment of fresh goods which has always been believed to be one of the areas where traditional supermarkets hold an advantage.

The individual products held within each of the categories above offer the customer less variety but aim instead at providing a superior price/quality relationship. Lidl's strategy for achieving this goal is to carry a very large percentage of private labels which are produced for them directly rather than holding brand names such as 'Gillette' razor blades, 'Kellogg's' cereal and 'Heinz' tomato ketchup. As mentioned earlier, it is assumed that the production of private labels can reduce costs up to 20 % which can be passed on to the customer in terms of lower prices. The percentage of private label products at Lidl constitutes 85 % of total products carried resulting in the opportunity to offer nearly all products at a lower price. This, paired with their reputation for driving a hard bargain when negotiating with suppliers of branded products, given their opportunity to buy in large quantities should, other things being equal, lead to a price level below that of traditional grocery retailers.

Lidl advocates simplicity throughout their stores by having broad aisles for easy access and presenting the goods in a bulk manner on pallets, as opposed to the meticulous shelf presentation used by super- and hypermarkets. Displaying articles in this manner and in many cases still packed in cartons, e.g. beverages, encourages the customer to purchase larger quantities of a particular product, which could be one factor driving the larger sale per square meter. This, combined with their limited assortment, provides easy access for not only getting stock to store in a rapid fashion but also for the customer who can easily orient him or herself in the store and find quickly what is needed. It is argued that this combination accelerates the time spend in the shop by an individual customer, which in turn increases the potential through flow of customers and thus the turnover.

It can be argued that the customer in such a set-up assists with the unwrapping of goods if, for example, they do not wish to buy a full carton of beverages, and as such takes on the role of an additional shop assistant. This naturally reduces the amount of required staff and the associated costs.

Product marketing characteristics

Whether or not the secretiveness of Lidl is an intended media strategy, which one could easily be led to assume, it works in their favor. The hype generated when Lidl is considering entry to a new market leaves the consumer with a perception of Lidl as a price leader. This, combined with their constant use of promotional campaigns on selected articles such as beverages, allows Lidl to fuel this perception effectively.

The use of price as a tactical weapon

Price is obviously one of the key parameters for Lidl and their discount strategy as no one wishes to pay a high price for a discount product. Whether Lidl's philosophy 'Best quality at the lowest price' can be proven beyond any doubt remains in question, but there is little doubt that the customer perceives Lidl as offering a similar quality at a lower price. In other words, the price/quality ratio at Lidl is perceived to be better than that of traditional supermarkets.

AC Nielsen has conducted a survey aiming at identifying whether it was households with a lower income that made up the bulk of buyers at a discount store and found that higher income households were strongly represented. A breakdown of the various income classes found shopping in a discount store is shown in Figure 5.11.

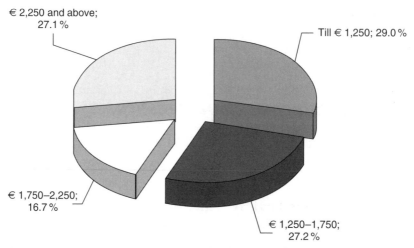

Figure 5.11   Net income distribution of households buying at discount

This indicates that those who could afford to shop at traditional super- and hypermarkets also shop at Lidl, and, unless driven by some unnatural desire, perceive the offerings at Lidl to hold better value on certain items.

Active leadership in price wars

Ever since Lidl decided to mirror the strategy of Aldi these two have been in constant battle within Germany, and it is believed that either Lidl or Aldi initiates the majority of price wars taking place there. However, this is not the only place where they gear up for battle.

Upon entering a new market, Lidl will initiate a price war in order to become established quickly on the particular market and to signal to the public that a store has opened, offering similar goods at lower prices. In Lidl's case they even claim to offer the 'Best quality at the lowest price', a statement which should induce an influx of customers to their stores. They seek to maintain this leadership, or the perception of such, through additional promotional campaigns aimed at, i.e. beverages, confectionary, and frozen foods which are where they have their stronghold.

This focus on simplicity, efficiency and passing on savings to the customer has gained Lidl a place among the European élite in terms of sales. It has furthermore, along with Aldi, exported what was formerly a purely German phenomenon to the entire European continent and has done so while creating a strong and feared brand.

Results – top of the class

As mentioned above, the Schwarz Group with Lidl as the corner stone is among the European élite of grocery retailers in terms of sales. In Planet Retail's 2003 ranking of the top 30 grocery retailers, Lidl held the spot of number 7 with estimated net sales of € 29.5 billion, holding a European market share of 3.4 % and closing in on Aldi's 3.5 % market share [18]. The latter point is emphasized by the growth rates enjoyed by the Schwarz Group and Lidl measured in percentage change in sales and percentage change in store numbers, which is shown in comparison to the other players in the grocery retail map which is illustrated in Figure 5.12.

On top of this impressive growth, estimates calculated by McKinsey and shown in Figure 5.13, provide a clear indication of Lidl's strength compared to the traditional super- and

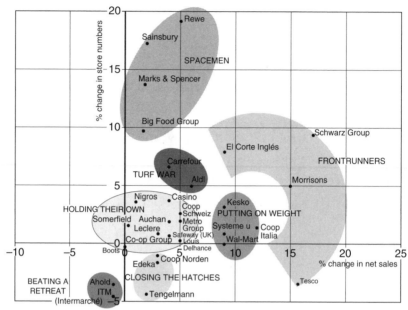

Note: Net sales growth calculated in local currency
Source: M+M planet Retail = www.planet/retail.net

Figure 5.12 Top 30 growth trends

	Lidl	Traditional supermarkets
EBIT % of Sales	6.7	3.0
Gross Profit per m^2	€ 955	€ 890
Staff cost % of Sales	5.6	13.1
ROIC %	11.8	2.7

Figure 5.13 Key financial ratios for Lidl as estimated by McKinsey

hypermarkets. During that year they were surpassed by Aldi on some of the key financial ratios but staggering growth may have turned the tables, paving the way for Lidl to take up the position as Europe's undisputed heavyweight champion of the discount grocery retail industry.

There can remain little doubt that there is nothing *little* about Lidl or the fact that German discount has swept the European grocery retail continent since the early 90's. What has this meant for the European grocery market as a whole?

Perspectives

Since the first self-service store saw the light of day in the 50's a great deal has happened within the grocery retail industry. Multi-counter supermarkets were the next step after self-service which were followed quickly by even bigger hypermarkets providing a one-stop-shopping experience for customers. The latest concept in this family tree were the discount stores which were introduced in the early 70's, based on the idea that a limited amount of articles would cover nearly 80 % of the grocery spending of a single household. Up until the Single European Market became a reality in the early 80's, grocery retail was confined by national boundaries. However, by the late 80's and throughout the 90's this has changed dramatically with all types of the above mentioned retail concepts and those championing them spreading across national borders.

Said to be the choice of the generation born in the 40's and 50's the super- and hypermarkets have been challenged by the discount chains which through efficiency, simplicity and innovative methods can offer articles at equal quality but at lower prices. These stores and Lidl in particular, are enjoying tremendous growth and demonstrate superior financial performance compared to the traditional super- and hypermarkets. It is believed that this trend will continue given new attitudes among customers in today's grocery jungle. They no longer perceive the discount store as a shameful place to do their shopping.

The impact of Lidl will force other players to evaluate their business models in order to compete and maintain their foothold. Lidl has managed to stir up the waters of an industry not only by its cost leadership but also through a strong brand and a unique approach to the experience of grocery shopping.

Lidl and other market players pursuing a discount strategy will continue to challenge the 'old' incumbents. A number of them are faced with a Gordian Knot when they are attacked by the discount grocery retailers offering both high quality and low cost. Lowering their prices will hit their margins due to their limited ability to lower their cost base. This strategic industry logic will therefore tend to galvanize the future success of the prudent discount grocery retailer.

6

Ryanair

Reshaping a competitive market through a consistent discount strategy

If you pile it high and sell it cheap, people will come to you.

Michael O'Leary, Chief Executive Officer, Ryanair

Flying with the giants

In the mid-80s when the airline industry was still highly regulated, Ryanair was established in order to provide an alternative to the flag carriers serving the Ireland-England route. In 1991, after five years of commercial operation, Ryanair was on the brink of bankruptcy and only a last minute transfer of funds from the Ryan family kept the company alive. On the back of this and inspired by Southwest Airlines, the company adopted and executed a discount strategy, which helped turn the company around. Through a consistent approach to the discount strategy, Ryanair did not only reach year on year profitability but also reshaped the European airline industry as a whole.

The story of Ryanair is therefore not just the story of a small independent airline that initially experienced difficulties in flying with the giant flag carriers but turned in time into a market leader. It is also the story of a company which had, and still has, a large impact on the environment in which it operates.

The airline industry – liberalized to full competition

Over the past two decades, the airline industry has experienced tremendous changes through the liberalization of the European skies. This liberalization was initiated in 1987 and was 10 years in the making before the market had become completely liberalized and could be characterized by full competition.

The deregulation of the airline industry came about in three packages of which the two first packages, introduced in 1987 and 1990 respectively, were aimed at establishing areas of free pricing as well as abolishing the 50/50 split of capacity on a route (see the timetable in Figure 6.1). This split was controlled previously by the flag carriers such as British Airways, Aer Lingus and Air France. The third package introduced in 1993, which came fully into effect by 1997, provided the opportunity for any EU commercial carrier to establish itself in any EU country, to provide service between any EU city, and to price freely under the proviso that no predatory pricing was used.

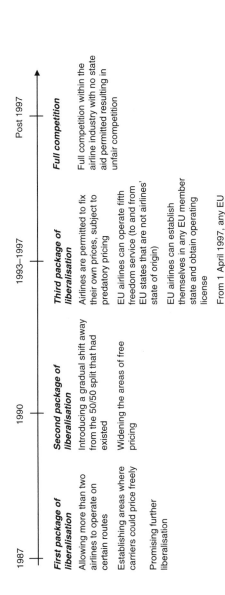

1987	1990	1993–1997	Post 1997
First package of liberalisation	*Second package of liberalisation*	*Third package of liberalisation*	*Full competition*
Allowing more than two airlines to operate on certain routes	Introducing a gradual shift away from the 50/50 split that had existed	Airlines are permitted to fix their own prices, subject to predatory pricing	Full competition within the airline industry with no state aid permitted resulting in unfair competition
Establishing areas where carriers could price freely	Widening the areas of free pricing	EU airlines can operate fifth freedom service (to and from EU states that are not airlines' state of origin)	
Promising further liberalisation		EU airlines can establish themselves in any EU member state and obtain operating license	
		From 1 April 1997, any EU Airline could operate any domestic route within any member state	

Figure 6.1 Airline industry timetable

The early days of deregulation

When Ryanair was established in the airline passenger traffic sector in Ireland in 1985, the airline industry was still highly regulated with national quotas on flight capacity and fixed prices [1]. In practice this meant that on any route between two countries, i.e. London Heathrow, UK, and Dublin, Ireland only two carriers were allowed to operate. The service between these two primary airports was allocated to the national flag carriers, British Airways and Air Lingus. This allowed the two national flag carriers to operate a duopoly up until 1987 when the liberalization of the industry began.

Despite this duopoly, Ryanair commenced services between secondary airports such as Waterford in the southeast of Ireland and London Gatwick and between Dublin and Luton, another secondary London airport, taking up some competition with the two flag carriers, British Airways and Aer Lingus, on the Dublin-London route, which was considered to be profitable. In contrast to the two flag carriers, Ryanair went to market with a simple fare structure with few or no restrictions, pricing their service at IR£ 98. This spawned a price reduction in fares at BA and Aer Lingus, who subsequently priced their lowest restricted fare at IR£ 95. To great astonishment at the Aer Lingus headquarters, Ryanair countered this by offering an unrestricted fare at IR£ 94.95 which was considered by Aer Lingus officials as 'predatory pricing to take over market share' and furthermore unsustainable. By 1989 customers could find fares priced at IR£ 70 for the service between Dublin and London [2].

As Ryanair expanded their route network on the back of the initial liberalization, Aer Lingus responded by lowering their prices by up to 50 % thus participating actively in the price war. This war, combined with advertisements by Ryanair, created the attitude among customers that Ryanair was the airline battling the establishment. One of these ads created by Ryanair congratulated Aer Lingus on their 50th birthday, showing a birthday cake of which a slice had been taken out.

Towards the liberalized sky with a new strategy

Upon adopting a 'No Frills, Low Cost' strategy, Ryanair continued to challenge the British establishment during the period from 1991 to 1997 whereas both BA and Aer Lingus continued down the strategic path of 'Full Fare, Value Adding' carriers. The strategy of Ryanair, however, proved to be the more successful, leading to them celebrating their 10th anniversary in 1995 as the biggest airline on every route they operated and carrying the largest number of passengers between Dublin and London that year.

As the airline industry had become completely deregulated by 1997, the battle between Ryanair and other British carriers was expanded and Ryanair turned their attention towards the Continent.

The final liberalization of the airline industry was particularly beneficial for the non-flag carriers who saw opportunities to compete with the flag carriers and gain a slice of the cake. Other low cost airlines emerged, such as easyJet, which commenced operations out of the UK in 1995 and Virgin Express which commenced operations in 1996 flying out of Brussels. These two and Ryanair were in sharp contrast to the flag carriers of the European Union member states, and a polarization of the industry began with the flag carriers operating a 'Full Fare, Value Added' strategy, on the one hand, and the 'No Frills, Low Cost' airlines on the other. The strategic response from the flag carriers to these new low cost sharks was initially to pool their resources and networks through the creation of alliances and the foundation of four major alliances took place in 1997.

The airline industry, therefore, was no longer one industry but instead a divided industry where one set of carriers, predominantly the flag carriers, were focusing on intercontinental services and establishing alliances, and the low cost airlines were focusing on point-to-point travel on intra-European routes. Despite this divide and perhaps as a protective measure against these new airlines, some flag carriers attempted to play both strategies by creating subsidiaries focusing on low cost and point-to-point travel. The most well-known of these are probably Go-Fly, a subsidiary of BA, and Buzz which was set up by KLM although operating out of the UK. However, the hard times that hit the airline industry following the 11th September terror attacks, reducing the number of passengers, and the subsequent war in Iraq pressurizing oil prices resulted in financial crisis and consolidation in the airline industry. The Belgian flag carrier Sabena filed for bankruptcy in 2001 and the airlines Go-Fly and Buzz were acquired by easyJet and Ryanair in 2003.

A transformed and polarized industry

A complete transformation of the airline industry had taken place in the course of 10 years with the alliances consisting of mainly flag carriers at one end of the spectrum and the low cost airlines at the other. This development is shown in Figure 6.2. In addition to this, an overwhelming amount of new airlines pursuing the no-frills-strategy emerged on the scene in the later years thus intensifying the competition even further on the European stage. This development is unlikely to diminish given the addition of 10 new countries to the European Community and with more to be added in the near future.

Is the 'No Frills, Low Cost' strategy a recipe for guaranteed success within the European airline industry or is there more to it than that?

When viewing the net margins over the past five years of some of the contenders who have played the game since deregulation was in its infancy, it becomes clear that the strategy is not necessarily a safe path to success. An example of this is Virgin Express which commenced services in 1996 and as such held the privilege of being one of the first in the market. It shows negative net margins in three of the five years displayed in Figure 6.3.

Ryanair, on the other hand, has been outperforming the initial competitors, the establishment, BA and Aer Lingus, as well as its nearest low cost rival easyJet year on year.

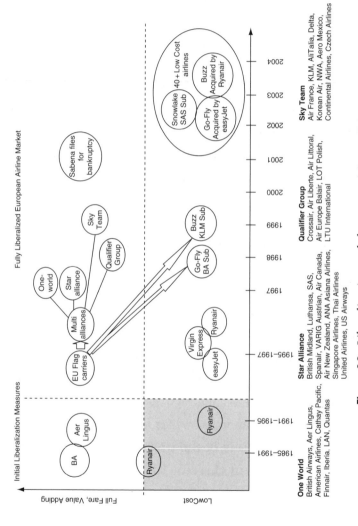

Figure 6.2 Liberalization and the competitive position

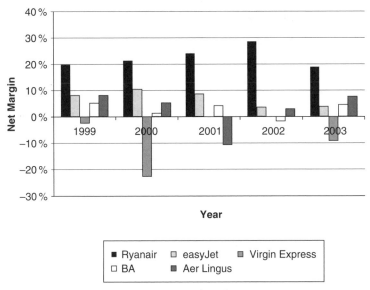

Figure 6.3 Financial performance

The success of Ryanair, therefore, is not the story of David slaying Goliath with a single throw of a stone or any single measure, but rather a story of a company which has reshaped the industry through innovation and focus. Over nearly two decades, Ryanair has managed to decrease the fares paid by Intra-European travellers whilst at the same time executing their strategy in a formidable manner, thinking up new ways to create revenue streams in an industry which was hibernating behind shelters of legislation. It is the story of a company which initiated its operations based on a differentiation type of strategy, but faced with threatening losses, migrated successfully to a discount strategy.

What did this discount strategy entail and how was it implemented successfully?

Ryanair as the alternative independent carrier

At first, Ryanair was established as an alternative independent carrier to the two flag carriers, British Airways and Aer Lingus, serving the Ireland-London routes with the aim of differentiating themselves in two areas. Firstly, they would charge a simple single fare, and, secondly, they would seek to provide a better service than the two flag carriers.

With the two flag carriers offering a multitude of different fare structures on their London-Dublin routes ranging from unrestricted round-trip fares priced at more than IR£ 200 to restricted discount fares priced as low as IR£ 99, Ryanair offered a simple single fare with no restriction, which, when the Dublin-London, Gatwick route was commenced, was priced at IR£ 98.

The increased customer service would stem from the customers' perception of a more 'personal' service as the same set of employees would be responsible for ticketing, boarding and in-flight service. From the commercial launch in 1985 to 1987, and sparked by the license to operate jet aircraft, Ryanair expanded their operations to include services on routes with little existing traffic service by Aer Lingus as well as services to secondary Irish population centres such as Galway and Shannon.

The customers responded favorably to the simple fares and the total number of passengers flying into and out of Ireland rose from 1.85 million in 1985 to 4.2 million in 1987.

Financial collapse evaded at the 11th hour

Despite a growing number of passengers and the infusion of IR£ 20 million by Tony Ryan and others, Ryanair was by January 1991 facing a financial collapse. The rapid expansion had strained the company's management system, resulting in annual losses of approximately IR£ 5 million in the preceding years. Michael O'Leary expressed in an interview in 2000 that at that time *we had no control over money at all* [3].

Facing a payment due to Dublin Airport of IR£ 34,000 and no funds available, the management team of Ryanair gathered to evaluate the options at hand. The options considered included:

- shutting down the airline, avoiding further losses;

- adding a high-fare business class service;

- serving as a feeder airline to US carriers;

- cutting frills and fares dramatically, hoping to mimic the success of US carrier Southwest Airlines.

On that particular winter night in Ireland, the decision was taken to carry on the operations of the airline but under a different strategy. The strategy was to mimic closely the strategy of Southwest Airlines which was operating a 'No Frills, Low Cost' airline. Another infusion of cash from the

Ryan family allowed for the payment of the Dublin Airport authorities and the commercial airline Ryanair was saved at the 11th hour, and the first European 'No Frills, Low Cost' airline became a reality.

The no frills, low fare strategy – not just one route

The introduction of a discount strategy necessitated a complete change of the company. This was initiated in 1991.

New management

The first thing that was done was to promote Michael O'Leary from the position of Finance Director to Deputy Chief Executive of the struggling airline. The reason Michael O'Leary was offered this position was, according to Mr O'Leary himself, 'because no one else was left to take the position'. However, others in the management team cited his ability to focus on objectives as the main reason. Focus was indeed needed for the exercise of the cost savings that followed.

However, focus was not the only talent Michael O'Leary possessed as he would soon become the face of Ryanair achieving icon status through his battle against the Establishment, his controversial statements and straightforward attitude when interviewed by the press. Only one other executive in the airline industry can match the recognition enjoyed among the public when his name is spoken, and that is Sir Richard Branson (Virgin Group) whose name and reputation, however, has been built in other industries.

Michael O'Leary has built his reputation entirely within the airline industry and is viewed as the person who made air travel available to millions of people at affordable prices. From holding a position as a tax consultant at KPMG in the years 1984 to 1986, he ventured into property development and acted as a financial advisor for the Ryan family up until 1988 when he became the financial director for Ryanair. In 1991, when Ryanair was facing financial difficulties and a new strategy was agreed upon, he then took up the position as Deputy Chief Executive and later became the Chief Executive of Ryanair.

A good illustration of the straightforward nature of Michael O'Leary and the salty nature of his comments is found in the interview conducted by Graham Browley and later published in the *Financial Times* weekend edition in 2003, where certain key points of the airline industry is commented upon [4].

> Ryanair's strict no-refund policy is the source of most complaints: 'We don't fall all over ourselves if they ... say my granny fell ill. What part of no refund don't you understand? You are not getting a refund so fuck off.'
>
> On Jurgen Weber, Lufthansa's chief executive: 'Weber says Germans don't like low fares. How the fuck does he know? He's never offered them any. The Germans will crawl bollock-naked over broken glass to get them.'

On co-existence with British Airways: 'There is too much: 'we really admire our competitors'. All bollocks. Everyone wants to kick the shit out of everyone else. We want to beat the crap out of BA. They mean to kick the crap out of us.'

On being happy: 'They don't call us the fighting Irish for nothing. We have been the travel innovators of Europe! We built the roads and laid the rails. Now it's the airlines!'

On the ultimate goal: 'Free tickets. In a decade or so, airlines will pay travellers to distribute people around Europe. The airline industry is Tesco, is Ikea, is network TV in the way viewers watch for free and advertisers pay for access to them, is the Internet in the same way that websites earn money for delivering click-through traffic to other sites.'

The behavior and visibility of Michael O'Leary has clearly been instrumental in developing a perception among the public of Ryanair as the airline that has made travel available for the masses. For Michael O'Leary personally it has meant that he has reached the status of an icon within the airline industry and even harvested awards such as 'Airline Personality' awarded by Skytrax in 2003. Among the nominees for this prize one could find the CEO's of BA, Deutsche Lufthansa, JetBlue Airways and even Southwest Airlines, the airline which Ryanair initially looked to for inspiration. His impact is also recognized by those who are holding the reins at competing airlines as this quote from the chairman of BMI British Midland illustrates:

He is almost certainly one of the most successful leaders in the industry, with a unique business model, discipline and an extraordinary level of confidence.

Sir Michael Bishop, chairman, BMI British Midland

Cost cutting programs

After deciding on the new strategy, the previous focus on customer service was replaced by a passion to preserve and generate cash championed by Michael O'Leary. Free coffee and snacks onboard all Ryanair flights were eliminated, labor contracts were re-negotiated to reflect productivity, meal vouchers for passengers waiting for flights delayed due to bad weather were abolished and staff members brought pens from home because these were in short supply at the office.

From being a mere exercise in cost reduction, low-cost became a mantra for Ryanair and was developed and implemented across all areas of the business in the following years.

Productivity-based compensation schemes

At the point of turnaround in 1991, Ryanair re-negotiated all labor contracts into productivity-based pay schemes in order to increase efficiency. Furthermore, the wages of, e.g. flight attendants were divided into three components, partly on the basis of the number of flights flown, partly as a function of their duty free sales and lastly a portion of fixed salary. These wages schemes have been a key factor in the superior performance of Ryanair. One measure of this is the number of passengers on a yearly basis per Ryanair employee, which, when compared to the competitors, illustrates the efficiency with which Ryanair operates [5], as can be seen in Figure 6.4.

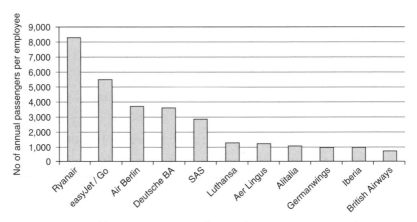

Figure 6.4 Efficiency in terms of annual passengers per employee

From the above one can derive that Ryanair manages to accommodate more than 10 times the amount of passengers per employee compared to BA and perhaps more notably, more than eight times that of Germanwings, another low cost operator. Ryanair employs mainly non-unionized staff, avoiding interference from labor organizations [6] and allowing for greater flexibility when negotiating the contractual terms for its employees.

In tandem with the wages schemes, the job responsibilities of personnel at Ryanair may cover multiple areas where, e.g. the same employee will conduct the ticketing, the boarding and the in-flight service. This flexibility of the employees is clearly beneficial to the entire process of accelerating the turnaround times for flights, resulting in less time on the ground and more flights per day.

Outsourcing to third parties

In all airports other than Dublin Airport, third party contractors are used for all ground operations. These include aircraft cleaning, baggage handling, ticketing and check-in. Contracts for such services are negotiated as multi-year contracts with private companies or airport authorities. The reasons for this are its more economical nature, the avoidance of employee relations and the added cost this may cause.

These contractors are also remunerated on the basis of their performance where, e.g. the contractors involved in ground operations they are rewarded if they meet the targeted turnaround time of 25 minutes and penalized if they fail.

The efficiency generated by such schemes is of paramount importance in order for Ryanair to not only keep their costs down but also to assure that the numbers of delayed flights are kept to a minimum. Delayed flights or punctuality is listed as one key variable leading to increased customer satisfaction with a low cost airline.

Re-organizing sales and distribution

The area of sales and distribution has been one of the main drivers of success for Ryanair as well as a widely publicized issue, namely the dislike Michael O'Leary holds for travel agents:

> Travel agents are a bloody waste of time.

In order to circumvent the high fees charged by travel agents, Ryanair established their own call center in Dublin where direct reservations were made by telephone. The overflow from the call center and incoming calls from Europe, after the service had been established to and from the continent, were routed to TeleTech UK, a third party which was paid on a per-call basis.

In 1997, Ryanair managed to reduce the commission fees paid to travel agents from the 9 % that was the industry standard to 7.5 %.

The immediate reaction to this move from certain groups of travel agents was to threaten Ryanair with a boycott. However, the Irish High Court prevented this, thus paving the way for a reduction in costs [7].

In 1999, Ryanair.com was launched to further reduce sales and distribution costs, as reservations could now be made directly by the customer through the company's website. Being one of the first companies along with easyJet to launch this method of booking air travel, Ryanair managed to make another leap ahead of its competitors and the traditional flag carriers, which at that point were still using call centers and the issuing of tickets. Within a year of introducing Ryanair.com as a vehicle for booking directly through the Internet, the website grew to take more than 50,000 bookings a week within three months and at year end accounted for roughly 40 % of all sales. By the end of 2001, direct sales from the Internet and the call center in Dublin accounted for 92 % of sales thus reducing the fees paid to travel agents to a minimum. The rapid growth of this distribution channel over the first 18 months is shown in Figure 6.5 [8].

Another slashing of costs was achieved with the introduction of Ryanair.com and a far reaching vehicle for marketing Ryanair's services was created at the same time. A vehicle which could communicate the latest offers in a matter of

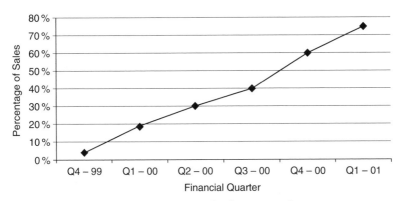

Figure 6.5 Internet booking growth

minutes, even seconds, and thus provide an unprecedented opportunity to react quickly to offers made by the competition. Only easyJet and Virgin Express introduced online booking earlier than Ryanair, whereas the traditional carriers, BA and Aer Lingus, introduced it years later and experienced a much slower growth than Ryanair [9].

Harmonizing and scrutinizing the fleet

In 1994, Ryanair initiated a complete shift of their fleet to consist of the Boeing 737 only. This allowed for cost savings on training of personnel and maintenance of aircraft while maximizing the flexibility of staff, as all routes were served by a similar type of aircraft. In 1998, Ryanair signed a contract for the delivery of 25 737-800s at a time of recession in the industry and therefore acquired the aircraft at bargain prices owing to other carriers' overcapacity and manufacturers' hard times. It is estimated that aircraft prices during a recession may drop to 50 % of the price during boom times.

In 1999, Ryanair's fleet consisted of 26 Boeing 737s, of which five were newly manufactured and part of the 25 aircraft deal struck with Boeing.

The remaining 20 aircraft were delivered between 2000 and 2003, and in 2002, Ryanair agreed to purchase an additional 100 aircraft manufactured by Boeing. This fleet of Boeing aircraft is equipped with the maximum number of seats and consist of one class only.

A recent measure to drive down the costs pertaining to the fleet further is to equip the Boeing aircrafts with non-reclining seats made of leather as this would reduce cost of repairing defect reclining seats [10], which ran at an esti-mated € 2.5 million, plus cleaning costs. A customer survey was conducted by Ryanair in which 20,000 of their passen-gers were asked whether they preferred the person in front of them having the ability to recline their seat. To no great surprise an overwhelming 94 % answered no. Window blinds, seat pockets and even the velcro headrests were also up for consideration as the elimination of these would generate addi-tional savings and potential revenue. The potential revenue would be in the form of replacing the velcro headrests with ones bearing the logo of advertisers, at a cost to those advertisers.

In addition, such measures could produce even faster turnaround times for aircraft owing to the lesser amount of cleaning needed. The targeted turnaround times are also a product of the secondary airports which Ryanair serves.

Customer care concept

Upon introducing the 'No Frills, Low Cost' strategy, Ryanair removed all in-flight amenities and focused on providing point-to-point travel for its customers, thus focusing on the transportation of passengers from point A to point B. This impacted on Ryanair's customer care concept as it was no longer a question of evaluating Ryanair on the basis of quality of the free coffee served or the amount of inches reserved for leg space, but instead it was a question of providing cheap travel. Given this, Ryanair identified a number of key variables which, they argue, are the cornerstone of customer service in today's airline business. Some of the key variables listed by Ryanair are: low prices, punctuality and efficient uncrowded airports.

These are different from those posted by traditional flag carriers to a significant degree, which usually cover the reach of network, airport lounges and in-flight amenities. Additionally, they fit the strategy of Ryanair's use of secondary airports, low turnaround times and a single model of aircraft.

This underlines the all encompassing nature of the low cost strategy and the success with which Ryanair has implemented this across the business.

However, in the quest for reducing costs some areas of customer care have suffered. One example is the use of metal stairs instead of 'air bridges' resulting in passengers having to board the airplane via those stairs, making travel for disabled people with Ryanair very difficult. Another aspect of customer service for which Ryanair has received bad publicity for is the misleading naming of certain destinations such as when the service to Malmø Sturup, in its infancy, was proclaimed to land in Copenhagen. Malmø Sturup is 70 kilometres outside of Copenhagen, not to mention that it is in Sweden and not in Denmark.

Despite these inconveniences, Ryanair has managed to stay free of too much damaging publicity and attract a growing number of passengers who are looking for the cheapest way to travel by air. When viewing two of the self-proclaimed variables for customer service, lowest price and punctuality, in 2003, Ryanair fares much better than their immediate competitors, as illustrated in Figure 6.6 and Figure 6.7 [12].

Looking at these two variables alone indicates that Ryanair can offer the lowest ticket prices on average and the best

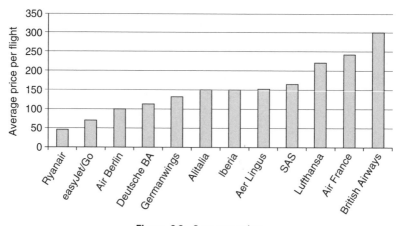

Figure 6.6 Lowest price

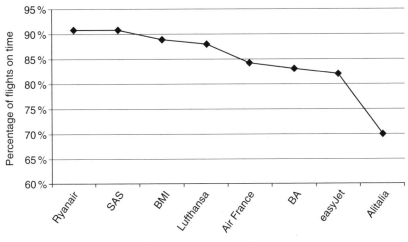

Figure 6.7 Punctuality

performance when it comes to punctuality. These statistics will almost certainly sit well with the European passengers on short haul distances for whom the number one priority is to get there on time and as cheaply as possible. These statistics also indicate the efficiency at which Ryanair operates given that their superior on-time performance does not raise the costs incurred by the airline and the fare paid by the passengers through higher ticket fares.

Apart from price and punctuality, the general service offered to travellers with Ryanair has gained the company both negative and positive publicity, which the following quotes from travellers illustrate [13]:

Ryanair – by Tapani Utunen

5 January 2005

'Tampere-Frankfurt/Hahn on November 26 and the same leg back on November 29, 2004. I was surprised: flights were 15 minutes ahead of schedule. Planes were rather new B737-800's, service was OK plus the Hahn airport quite modern and clean. No complaints really! I saved a good amount of euros and spent them in Germany instead'.

Ryanair by Hans de Witte

20 December 2004

'Arriving 2 minutes too late because of the traffic on the road and bad weather, for a flight from Weese (D) to Girona (42 minutes before departure time) the desk lady told us that we could not leave. And with us another 10/12 persons. After a long and intensive research she showed us that in the 'small notices' this was mentioned and via Internet agreed by us. Officially they are right but a bit of tolerance would be a better PR point. This bad experience was so frustrating! To make the disaster complete, the plane left 15 minutes too late! Our first and last Ryanair flight.'

Dozens of similar quotes can be found illustrating both satisfied and dissatisfied customers but the fact remains that Ryanair has enlarged their business to a leading brand within European aviation.

New brand and branding

The brand and branding of Ryanair after the decision to implement the new strategy changed in order to promote the low fare concept. This included the Ryanair branding of themselves as the 'Low fares airline' and advertising campaigns focusing heavily on the price difference between the fares found at Ryanair and those charged by both traditional flag carriers and other low cost airlines such as easyJet.

When the Internet was introduced as a booking vehicle in late 1999, Ryanair went into a sponsorship contract with Sky-News Weather, a program broadcast throughout Europe, which allowed Ryanair to promote Ryanair.com as the premier location on the web for low fares in Europe. In order to back these words up by action, Ryanair introduced what was known as 'lowest fare guarantee' which stated that anyone who could find a lower fare on any other Internet site with a similar itinerary would be paid twice the fare by Ryanair.

From that dark winter night in 1991, when Ryanair was virtually unknown to most European travellers, to the present it has generated a brand that is synonymous with low fare travel and known throughout Europe.

Political mass marketing

From the early days of Ryanair's new low cost strategy, the advertising campaigns have been of a provocative nature, which, combined with the extrovert nature and the comments of Michael O'Leary, have brought it great publicity.

One example of this is the advert, mentioned earlier, congratulating Aer Lingus on their 50th birthday, showing a picture of a birthday cake where a slice has been carved out. In addition to taking on their direct competitors in advertising, Ryanair also attacked what they called the Establishment, lashing out at the outrageous taxes travellers were paying, through another advert which read 'Dublin–London only IR£ 19.95 . . . and that includes the ridiculous taxes'. Another controversial advertisement resulted in BA suing

Ryanair in 2000 over trademark infringement and malicious falsehood due to an advert which not only stated that the fares charged by Ryanair were five times lower than those charged by BA but did so under the headings *'Expensive BA'* and *'Expensive Ba—ds'*. The High Court in London ruled in favor of Ryanair with the Judge describing the campaign as 'honest, comparative advertising'. A significant ruling, which prompted Michael O'Leary to respond with the following diplomatic yet scathing comment:

> I would like to thank BA for taking this action to prove what everybody already knows – that they are expensive.

Other examples of Ryanair advertising campaigns, which can be said to be provocative and bordering on the limits of good taste, include those where the Belgian symbol, Manneken Piss, was used against Sabena Airlines, the Pope was used to promote the fact that Ryanair.com is the only airline guaranteeing the lowest fares on the Internet and the former Information Minister of Iraq, who was seen on TV in the early days of the Iraq war proclaiming that Iraq had defeated the Allied forces, was displayed as the Head of Information for easyJet, proclaiming they offer the lowest fares (see Figure 6.8).

Figure 6.8 Examples of adverts disseminated by Ryanair

Apart from generating publicity the adverts were also considered rather amusing by the general public, the key target group for Ryanair, and fostered the perception that they truly were the airline offering the lowest fares.

On a less amusing note, Ryanair has recently been involved in another court case in which the European Commission ruled that they had received illegal aid from Belgium's Wallonia regional government, which owns Charleroi airport [14]. The result was that Ryanair was to repay €4 million out of the €16 million it had received in aid. Additional allegations have emerged from Iberia, which is in the process of collecting information to prove that Ryanair has received similar illegal aid at other airports.

Another court case, concerning the charge that Ryanair demanded for providing wheelchairs to the disabled, has come to an end with the ruling that such must be provided by the carrier. This has led Ryanair to increase all fares by €0.50 to cover these costs.

Active price leadership

Given that Ryanair creates adverts and attempts to manipulate the public media with the intention of increasing the perception of Ryanair as the carrier offering the lowest prices, active leadership in terms of low prices must also be maintained.

Ryanair therefore monitors the prices offered in the market constantly to ensure that no other airline can match its low prices. Besides this it enters new routes by setting fares at 50 % of their previous levels to not only capture market share but also to fuel the perception of Ryanair as the airline with the lowest prices.

An extreme measure where tickets are actually given away is another tool used by Ryanair to enhance the perception of low fares.

Ryanair's discount product – cheaper and better

Upon the adoption of the 'No Frills, Low Cost' strategy Ryanair successfully implemented a number of cost cutting initiatives in order to support the discount strategy, but what did that entail for the product itself? What does a discount air travel product look like?

The core product itself, being transporting a person from point A to point B via air, is no different from the standard product offered by the full fare product offered by the flag carriers. However, all surrounding services such as in flight amenities, airport lounges and assigned seats are stripped away and turned into revenue streams, as the passengers can purchase some of these. This leaves the core product much like that of a ride on a bus, albeit a sophisticated bus travelling in the sky. The main differences in the later years are the new ways in which the product is produced and distributed.

Product production characteristics

Being a discount product it is based on the principle of simplicity and in the case of Ryanair its simple point-to-point fare structures are in sharp contrast to those offered by the traditional flag carriers. The product of Ryanair is as simple as it can be as it only covers transportation from A to B as opposed to the wide variety of fare structures offered by the traditional flag carriers, ranging from business class to low price fares where departure dates are normally restricted.

The simplicity of Ryanair's fares can therefore be characterized by a 'lean' structure where all extra services, such as free coffee, snacks, airport lounges or assigned seats, are stripped off the product. Other low cost airlines such as Debonair, which didn't survive, experienced grave difficulties when attempting to add such extras to the product, as the business model couldn't bear these.

Many carriers construct their offerings in order to retain their customers with the predominant method being frequent flyer programs offering either a discount on the fare or access to the business lounges of that particular airline. Ryanair has no such thing since the fare itself is one of the lowest in the market, if not the lowest, and lounges are non existent. The loyalty of customers is gained through a consistent low price, a simple fare structure as well as superior on-time performance.

When Ryanair launched its website, Ryanair.com, in late 1999 the entire process of booking or producing the product of one air fare was in essence handed over to the customer.

The customer navigates the website and searches for available flights and prices, books the one desired and pays online by credit card. This not only increases efficiency and productivity for Ryanair but also allows the customers to book their tickets in their own time reducing the waiting time one might have to endure when calling a travel agent or the Ryanair call center. Upon successful completion of buying a ticket through the website, the customer is given a reference number which acts as the ticket, thus further reducing the cost and adding to the simplicity the customer enjoys by not having to go through the mail on a daily basis to ensure that the ticket has arrived in time for the flight.

As mentioned previously, customers booking their tickets online are asked to pay instantaneously by means of credit card and this implies that Ryanair does not have to worry about customers not being able to pay their fare once booked. Cash is generated prior to the service being provided leading to a positive cash flow impact.

The customer care part of the discount air travel product is, as mentioned earlier, made up of several factors with on-time performance, guaranteed low prices and low percentage of lost bags being key according to Ryanair themselves. The efficiency with which Ryanair has been able to operate after implementing its discount strategy in 1991 has resulted in superior performance on these variables. In addition to this, the expectations of customers have effectively been lowered given the outright labelling of the product as a no nonsense point-to-point discount product, and the actual performance of Ryanair has more than met those expectations. In fact they are considered 'best in class' on all three variables when compared to their immediate competitors.

The product development of a simple fare, discount air travel product can be said to consist of the number of destinations served by that particular air line. In the case of Ryanair, their rapid expansion into the Continent has been overwhelming, to say the least, as they have expanded their network from a handful of routes in 1995 to 209 routes covering 93 destinations across 19 European countries from no less than 12 bases. Many of these destinations have come under criticism from competitors as they consist largely of secondary airports which in some cases are situated many kilometres outside the city center they claim to transport their passengers to.

Examples of these remotely placed airports are Frankfurt (Hahn) which is a two hour bus drive from the center of Frankfurt, and Malmø Sturup which is roughly 50 kilometres' from the center of Malmø. This latter service was marketed initially as Stansted–Copenhagen but given the fact that Copenhagen, as mentioned earlier, is not only a 70 kilometre drive from Malmø Sturup, but is situated in Denmark and not in Sweden, led to criticism of this labelling and Ryanair was forced to relabel.

Product marketing characteristics

For Ryanair, the introduction of a discount product has turned out to be an almost sufficient criterion for success despite the fact that conventional marketing theory stipulates brand as the key. In order to establish the brand, considerable effort and cost are usually expended on marketing. In the case of Ryanair, this amount has been very limited.

Since the introduction of Ryanair.com, the majority of sales are executed through the Internet and with the Internet penetration of many western European countries, rising to 80 % or above, nearly all potential customers can be reached. This results in a large portion of marketing actually being delivered through the Internet via its website, rendering this almost free of charge.

This, combined with the ability of Ryanair and particularly Michael O'Leary to obtain column space in several publications as well as having some of their court cases shown during prime time on television, has resulted in Ryanair spending significantly less on marketing than their competitors.

The use of price as a tactical weapon

It is no surprise that one of the key areas when following a discount strategy is to use price as a tactical weapon. This entails that prices are kept at a certain level but also relates to the marketing as such and the perception generated among the customers. In a market characterized by full competition one must also pay constant attention to the moves of one's competitors in order to maintain control of the contingencies of price wars.

The customers' perception of price

There is little doubt that Ryanair has managed to create a perception among the European travellers that it is indeed the cheapest airline. This has been achieved through consistent marketing on price to such an aggressive extent that one could argue that this marketing has been an all out attack on the Establishment and the high fares charged by the full fare carriers.

This perception, leading to attitudes such as 'Ryanair is the cheapest and they will keep on battling to stay cheapest', creates a faith among travellers that Ryanair will continue to offer the cheapest going rate. Through this, the loyalty of customers is gained, and new customers are snatched from competing carriers.

Price perception is emphasized by the following examples of customers' reaction to the travel experience:

Dear Sir,

I would like to complain bitterly about the cost and service of your airline on a recent trip to Turin!

Firstly the cost was £6 return and secondly, for this, we had to endure flights on a brand new 737-800. The cabin crew were totally efficient and friendly and the pilots utterly professional.

This is outrageous behavior from a low cost airline!! How can people (who think they are better than everyone else) justify flying with BA paying hundreds of pounds more for the same services (minus a sandwich)??!!

If you continue in this manner I will have no option but to report you to the CAA!!

Yours Sincerely

Jeff Swift, Leeds
17th July 01.

To: Mr Michael O'Leary, Ryanair

cc: Mr Rod Eddington, British Airways

Dear Mr O'Leary,

I've just returned from a business trip to Dublin and flew Ryanair for the first time. Both flights were on time, very pleasant crew, a good experience.

Cost **£39.18 with Ryanair.** Equivalent similar timed flights **on British Airways £300.40** (yes £300.40!!!). Needless to say should I be travelling to Dublin again I'll be flying Ryanair. It's a pity that you currently don't operate any other routes out of LBA (or MAN) – here's hoping. Wishing you and all at Ryanair continued success.

Yours faithfully

Nigel Owen
June 24th 2002.

Leading the price wars

From the very beginning in 1991, Ryanair has assumed a clear leadership in price wars by opening their competing route between Dublin–London at fares below those of the two flag carriers, BA and Aer Lingus. As mentioned previously, the reaction from Aer Lingus to the prices charged by Ryanair was considered as unsustainable even at an early stage. The price has since been lowered significantly.

From the outset, the fare between Dublin and London was priced at IR£ 94.95 but after the implementation of the discount strategy the average fare paid by Ryanair travellers has been declining from around € 70 towards € 45 and as such less than a third of that believed to be unsustainable.

The strategic goal of Ryanair in terms of pricing was, and still is, to keep their prices at least 10 % lower than other airlines operating the same or a similar route.

In addition to the consistent approach of offering the lowest available prices, Michael O'Leary and his much debated view on the future of air fares, which he anticipates will become free of charge, emphasizes the role of Ryanair as the price leader.

Results – Best in class

It is hard to argue with the fact that the turnaround of Ryanair, by way of a consistent discount strategy, has been effective in financial terms. But could other strategic methods lead to equally impressive results?

In terms of the profit and loss accounts, the deficit experienced in 1991, where the company was on the brink of bankruptcy, has been turned into sustained year on year profits since the implementation of the discount strategy. Ryanair is indeed an impressive acquaintance in today's airline business, displaying net margins of roughly 20 %

over the past five years in an industry where many of the major airlines are struggling to even produce a positive result.

In terms of growth, the number of passengers carried by Ryanair has grown from 2.5 million in 1995 to an astonishing 21.4 million in 2003 equalling a growth of 856 % in less than 10 years.

The growth in market share experienced on key routes over the past two years also bears witness to a successful business and that on the back of consolidation among the flag carriers and casualties such as Sabena airlines. The growth on selected routes is displayed in Figure 6.9.

None of the other players in the market can display similar figures and although Ryanair is not yet the largest airline in Europe it is without doubt the most profitable. In addition to this, they seem well positioned to continue their hunt for other scalps in the industry through continued expansion of their route network while executing the low cost strategy to perfection.

	Market share in 2002	Market share in 2004
London–Dublin	39 %	46%
London–Stockholm	30 %	38 %
London–Rome	20 %	35 %
London–Milan	21 %	37 %
London–Hamburg	22 %	34 %
London–Berlin	0 %	34 %

Figure 6.9 Growth on selected routes

Perspectives – a revolution in the airline industry?

Since the introduction of the 'No Frills, Low Cost' business model in Europe by Ryanair and the liberalization of the skies, the industry has gone through tremendous changes. Having once been ruled by the giant flag carriers, the industry has been hit with meteoric impact by the discount strategy, causing the dinosaurs of the industry to tremble and in certain cases to lose out completely.

The industry itself has experienced a polarization between 'Full Fare' and 'Discount' where the former is reserved primarily for the flag carriers who, in order to retaliate, have formed alliances and networks among not only European carriers but also American ones, as the intercontinental traffic remains their realm. This, however, does not alter the fact that on the European short haul market the discount carriers have claimed such significant ground through their effective strategy that flag carriers and other full fare airlines find it very hard to compete.

Even when BA and KLM tried to emulate the concept through their low fare airlines, Go-Fly and Buzz, they soon came to realize that this area was not one in which they held the expertise and they surrendered ultimately by selling them off to none other than easyJet and Ryanair.

In the wake of Ryanair and easyJet, a number of other low cost airlines have seen the light of day over the past five years but none can to this day mirror the success of particularly

Ryanair. Some of those, e.g. Debonair, have been forced to throw in the towel as their implementation and/or execution of the discount strategy have left them stranded in a fiercely competitive market.

What is the outlook for the market? Judging from the past eight years, the low cost airlines are gaining more and more of the market almost at an exponential rate with the market share held at the end of 2003 equal to 7 % [15] (see Figure 6.10).

Compared to the US where the market share held by low cost airlines is in the region of 25 %, there is still plenty of ground for the low cost airlines to capture, which, all else being equal, will result in further consolidation within the business and more casualties among the flag carriers.

The case of Ryanair therefore displays promising prospects for a discount strategy as the incumbent flag carriers will not be able to counteract the high quality of the core product

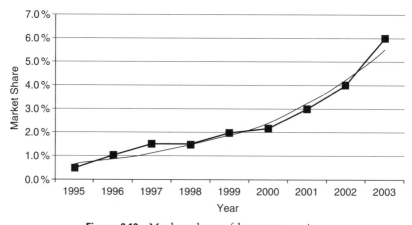

Figure 6.10 Market share of low cost carriers

combined with the low price. Ryanair and other successful discount carriers have all the hallmarks needed to take market share in the future: a good product produced at an unprecedented low level of cost, better service perception, a recognized and highly valued brand, customer support and a lean technology with easy ticketing, quick boarding and high turnaround rates.

7

The building blocks of a discount business strategy

Maturity and liberalization in different industries

The companies analysed represent three significantly different industries albeit with similar characteristics. All three industries have existed for some time and can be characterized as mature industries, mature industries which have experienced a continuous development initiated through both technological innovation and market pressure.

The airline passenger industry has seen a continued development of the aircraft and their range and capacity allowing for markets to become international. The telecommunications industry has experienced tremendous growth and innovation in terms of network and terminals allowing for multiple mobile services, such as SMS, MMS and 3G technologies to be marketed. The grocery retail industry may not have fostered as many innovations in a technological sense as the airline and telecommunication industries but the store format has gone through tremendous transformation owing to market pressures. From being dominated by local grocery retailers the industry now embraces a variety of concepts from specialty stores to hypermarkets.

Given this, the main similarities that can be established across all three industries are their mature nature, technological innovation and continued development. In addition, all of these industries have gone through a process of liberalization in the course of the past three decades. The passenger airline industry has gone from being a regulated monopoly ruled by the flag carriers to an industry characterized by full competition after liberalization came into effect in 1997. The telecommunications industry has travelled a similar path where the incumbent's former monopoly has been challenged through a growing number of newcomers entering the industry on the back of liberalization. Liberalization of the grocery retail industry pertains to the free movement of goods and the ruling that a product good enough for one EU country can be imported or exported to any other EU country and sold there. When the European Court of Justice ruled in favor of this in the 'Cassis de Dijon' case it effectively opened up the European market for grocery retail.

Combining the maturity and the liberalization of the three industries has resulted in the hypercompetitive nature which characterizes all three. These are all industries where entrenched incumbents have been challenged to adapt to new market forces and where new entrants are seeking to carve out a piece of the former monopoly's market share. A final competitive characteristic that the three companies share is the value destruction they have brought about in their wake.

As such the three examples all represent mature industries characterized by hypercompetitive market forces, which have been heavily impacted by the arrival of companies pursuing discount strategies.

Because of this, the playing field may be said to be similar for the three companies in terms of competitive forces whereas the industry drivers are significantly different.

Despite the inherent difference between the three industries in terms of their end-product, areas of a generic nature can be identified. It is precisely these areas which constitute the foundation of a discount strategy.

The building blocks of a 'discount strategy'

When seeking to identify areas of a generic nature across the three companies, the product offering itself offers an excellent starting point. In industries where diversification has been the mantra and the product offerings have grown increasingly complex, the companies analysed have all stripped their product offering down to the core product itself. Ryanair offers their passengers a one class fits all transport service from A to B stripped of all extras such as free coffee and lounges. CBB offers a single class pre-paid mobile service charged by the second and free of any subscription fees. Lidl doesn't offer a single product but instead a shopping experience where customers can find a limited assortment of good quality products displayed in bulk and priced very aggressively.

Given the simple and 'stripped' nature of the product offered by all three companies, the *Product* itself can be identified as the first building block of a discount strategy.

Having identified the *Product* as a first element, the positioning of such a product in the market, and how the three companies seek to brand themselves, becomes of interest. Again similarities are apparent across the three companies as they all seek to position their product as a product of equal or better quality but at lower, or even much lower, costs. A combination of diversification and cost leadership is pursued by all three entailing an immense focus on the price/quality ratio of their product. This positioning is, furthermore, emphasized through the branding of the companies themselves which all seek to establish a sense of 'us against them' or in two of the cases 'David against Goliath'. This signals to customers that they are attacking the very Establishment that thrived on overcharging its customers during the monopolistic days.

The aggressive price positioning and the notion of 'attacking the establishment for the good of the customer' can be seen in the branding of all three companies and as such *Brand* constitutes the second building block of a discount strategy.

With *Product* and *Brand* identified as generic elements, the focus turns toward the actual customer purchasing the discount product. Are there any similarities between the customers of Ryanair, CBB and Lidl? And if so what are they? There are indeed similarities as the concept of discount has grown from being the ugly duckling to becoming, if not the beautiful white swan, then a highly respected way of shopping. Some would even say that discount offers the customer a 'smart way of shopping' given that you are not paying for any more than you get. Many customers have become aware of this and are now seeking greater simplicity and transparency when shopping. And the discount product offers exactly that.

The *Customer* is the third building block of a discount strategy owing to a similar attitude towards discount shopping, which is held by customers across the three industries to which the analysed companies belong.

The last building block pertains to the technology and the delivery mechanisms deployed in the three companies and the choice of technology to support this. None of the three companies has achieved its success by implementing ground breaking technology or focusing on the latest and the greatest. Instead they have implemented technology which, at that point in time, had proven reliable and, above all, scalable. As such it is not a single piece of technology that constitutes the generic nature of technology but rather the place that technology holds within each company and the parameters used to choose a specific technology and/or production process.

Therefore, building block number four is labelled as *Technology* although covering a broader spectrum than, e.g. any one specific technology.

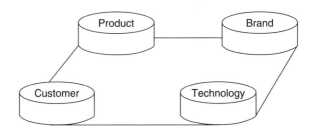

Figure 7.1   The four building blocks of a discount strategy

The four building blocks of a discount strategy, being *Product, Brand, Customer* and *Technology,* can be illustrated as shown in Figure 7.1.

The following elaborates on the characteristics of each and the similarities present across Ryanair, CBB Mobil and Lidl.

The product

The discount product obviously holds a highly important place as the strategic aim of all three companies can be described as:

> The ability to offer similar or better quality at lower prices.

Despite the simplistic nature of this purpose, achieving it is a different story altogether. The manner in which CBB, Ryanair and Lidl have achieved this aim shows significant similarities while opposing those tactics employed by entrenched competitors.

In a market where nearly all competitors were offering a variety of price packages, CBB introduced one simple offering equal for all and based on a single minute of usage price applicable 24 hours a day seven days a week. In addition to this single offering, much of the traditional customer service, such as billing and account information, was moved to an online environment where the customer could gain real-time information and control his or her account.

Ryanair made simple air travel from point A to B available in a market where traditional carriers bundled this travel service with, e.g. free coffee onboard, pre-assigned seats, hub connections and lounges. These auxiliary services are removed completely from the discount travel of Ryanair, which in fact operates more like a bus in the sky. A customer purchases a single-class ticket to travel from Dublin to London and receives just that and no more. A lean, simple and unbundled product which stands in sharp contrast to the myriad of ticket classes of the traditional flag carriers.

In the case of Lidl, the product relates more to the actual store concept rather than one specific product, and there can be little doubt that simplicity plays a large part both in terms of the assortment, the lay-out of stores and their design. The assortment is limited to those goods that have a high turnover generating high inventory turns and that are found in most households. Displayed in bulk manner along wide aisles simplifies the search for items signalling the simplicity and the no-nonsense nature of Lidl as the product. Adding private labels, which constitute more than 8 % of all goods, allows Lidl to pursue simplicity further in production.

In terms of generic product characteristics, *'no frills'*, *simplicity* and *lean nature*, which are central to the discount product, can be identified across all three companies.

The brand and the product itself show similar characteristics across the three companies but given the highly different nature of the end product, the generic nature of the customer appears hard to identify initially.

The brand

When looking at the brand of the three companies significant similarities exist in terms of how the individual companies are branding their product or service, the marketing tactics employed and how they seek to position themselves in the market.

This simplicity of the discount product is accompanied by a very aggressive price structure and marketing of the product. It has been of paramount importance to CBB, Ryanair and Lidl that the customer perceives their products or services as a superior offering in terms of price/quality value. CBB has reduced the minute charges from €0.23 to €0.09 within the space of two years in order to secure their position as a price leader. The position of price leadership has also been pursued relentlessly by Ryanair leading to, e.g. a reduction in fares on the Dublin-London route from €145.00 to €29.00 over a period of 15 years. In some cases Ryanair even gives tickets away for free in order to maintain its position as a price leader. Lidl has, throughout its existence, waged fierce price wars against their local rivals Aldi and in later years the growing number of European discount retailers. Recent studies show that the introduction of a Lidl store in the Nordic region in some cases has led to price reductions of nearly 20 % on certain items.

Price aggressiveness is but one branding characteristic that the three companies share. Others include the notion of 'us against them', which is being used throughout the marketing campaigns of all three companies. Ryanair attacks the traditional flag carriers via their provocative ad campaigns, CBB questions the position of the former monopoly TDC and its price structures and Lidl is taking on all grocery retailers through pure price aggressiveness and the mystique surrounding it.

The branding of all three revolves around being the cheapest alternative as the branding campaign of Ryanair being 'the low fares airline' and both CBB and Lidl being perceived as the price leaders within their respective markets illustrates. Being the cheapest alternative is however followed by outperforming traditional competitors on specific parameters such as on-time performance for Ryanair, real time billing and account information in the case of CBB and high quality low priced private label products manufactured and sold by Lidl.

The message of 'Equal or better quality at lower costs' as well as waging a war against the Establishment that has overcharged the majority of customers for far too long, appears to be the essence of discount branding.

The customers

Originally, the customers of discount products were viewed primarily as belonging to the lower income classes. However, a shift has occurred in shopping for discount products today. Currently, all income classes are represented among the customers of Ryanair, CBB and Lidl.

The idea of a single class of product, where no segmentation is made, appears to hold great value among customers as they focus on the value delivered and the ability to 'shop smart'. Combining this with the notion that all three companies actually do fare better on certain service related parameters, which appear to hold great significance with the customers, only emphasizes the fact that you do indeed 'shop smart' when discount shopping.

Product simplicity and the transparency that this breeds, as no multiple product classes are offered, also appears to sit well with the customers of a discount product. Customers actually value the fact that they are not made to pay for anything except the product itself. This challenges much of the literature on marketing and relationship management where additional auxiliary services are believed to build stronger ties with the customer, enhancing the probability of repeat purchases.

The discount product is a transaction based product, which doesn't seek to develop a variety of non-core auxiliary services but aims instead at satisfying the customers' need for good quality at low price. The focus on price/quality, rather than surrounding services, has been viewed favourably by customers who feel they are getting exactly what they pay for. This has resulted in a degree of loyalty as the three companies have come to be known as the price leaders or among those.

One feature that all three companies have adopted is to have the customer as a co-producer of the goods or services being offered. This has been received by the individual customers not as a nuisance but rather as a welcome service allowing all three companies to fare extremely well in terms of the service perceived. CBB offers real time billing and account information, Ryanair lets the customers search for flights online in their own time and Lidl has the customers unwrap the pallets, thus avoiding having to employ the manpower necessary to restock stores while allowing for more aisle space.

Customers have travelled a long way over the past two decades and are now concerned about 'shopping smart' and paying for what they want rather than what is in a total package of core product/service and auxiliary components.

Technology

The final building block pertains to the technology deployed by the three companies or rather the rationale behind the chosen technologies. Technology has not been the driving factor of any of the three companies but has instead been implemented with the notion of discount in mind.

Offering a 'No Frills' product, which is very lean in its nature, leads to a less complex value chain paving the way for choosing proven technology over state-of-the-art newly developed technology. Ryanair harmonized their fleet to consist of the Boeing 737 only, an aircraft that has proven its worth and for which trained personnel can be found. CBB and Ryanair shifted or introduced the Internet as the primary sales and customer service channel at a point where e-commerce was well tested and accepted among the buying public. Lidl not only compress the value chain by holding a limited assortment of goods but has also expanded its center of gravity through backward integration by producing their private label goods.

Technology in a discount sense is concerned about whether or not the technology will suit the discount value proposition rather than being the actual driver of the strategy. Given this, the self-service concept of all three is supported by the technological choices of Ryanair, CBB and Lidl with the first two utilizing the Internet for both sales and customer service related issues and Lidl designing their stores for easy access and bulky displays that require some self-service on the customer's part.

The four blocks as one discount strategy

With some additional light being shed on the four building blocks, the interlinked nature of all four cannot be underestimated as they, together, form the unity which comprises the heart of a discount strategy, as illustrated in Figure 7.2.

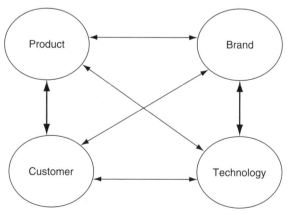

Figure 7.2 The interlinked nature of the four building blocks

The interconnected nature of the four building blocks requires that focus and consistency across all four must be maintained and balanced when aiming for simplicity and leanness. But which specific variables can be identified within each block as those that make the heart tick and the body grow strong?

8

The attractiveness of the core product

From peaceful coexistence to disruption

As emphasized earlier there are only two choices in the conventional literature on strategy: a company can either elect to be a differentiator or it can decide to pursue cost leadership. These two generic strategies fit well together in so far as companies adopting such strategies can live together in peaceful coexistence. However, much of the strategy thinking so far deals with the achievement of efficient competition.

No matter whether Adam Smith's invisible hand operates in a competitive or hypercompetitive environment, competition is viewed as a stable homeostasis, at least in the medium to long term. On the competitive field some fighting may take place but the winner does not take it all. There is always room for new entrants.

Even if a company has become a successful contender and arrived at the position of a clear winner with the largest market share, it still has to live in peaceful coexistence with the competitors. Prevailing competition and anti-trust legislation in most markets demands that the market leader behaves. If the market share reaches a certain level and the company gets a significant market share, direct or indirect public regulation comes into play in almost every economy today. This means that the highly successful company has to treat its competitors with the utmost care, such as avoiding pricing which may be perceived as predatory, having open access to distribution channels, and ensuring that anti-competitive behavior does not occur.

In case the invisible hand does not ensure peaceful coexistence, public regulation takes over and restores the imperfections so that harmful effects are rejected.

Business schools operate within this conventional framework and do not yet encapsulate strategizing which exceeds such borderlines. The typical Mr Company adopting and executing a discount strategy never went to business school and is consequently not aware of the inherent homeostasis.

When the successful execution of a discount strategy turns into disruption, there is no way to return to the past equilibrium. Values are not only being created, they are also being destroyed.

In one of the most alarming passages in Robert Kennedy's account of the Cuban Missile Crisis he expresses great concern over the possibility of a loss of control over events, a development which, it was felt, could precipitate a nuclear holocaust [1].

In fact, the successful execution of a discount strategy, appearing eventually as a disruptive business case, has many similarities with a loss of management control over the nuclear deterrent. Once the disruption commences, it just continues.

Disruption and the corresponding value destruction

The introduction of disruptive strategies can have significant consequences for the value attributed to an entire industry given the aggressive search for offering superior or equal quality at lower costs. Once the customer has been made aware of the existing discount products and their potentially superior price/quality ratio, pressure will begin to mount on the established players and the established pricing structures of the industry.

If we take a closer look at the European airline industry and the disruption the emergence of low fare airlines has brought with it, the potential value destruction must appear frightening to the established carriers. The difference between the average fare of, e.g. Ryanair, stated to be € 40, and the average fare of all the members of the Association of European Airlines (AEA), estimated at € 120, is a staggering € 90 [2]. This indicates a potential value destruction of nearly 60 %, equivalent to € 12.6 billion, of the current airfare turnover if the low fares

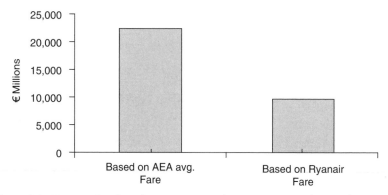

Figure 8.1 Potential value destruction in the European airline industry in 2004

promoted by Ryanair, EasyJet and others were implemented by the rest of the carriers.

Such value destruction, as depicted in Figure 8.1, of the entire airline industry is naturally dependant on passenger numbers remaining constant, which is not the case in real life. However, the increase in passengers that such a potential reduction in average fares will necessitate in order to maintain the total revenue is unlikely in the short-term.

Turning our attention to the mobile telephony industry we can identify a similar pattern with a significant reduction in minute of use prices promoted by the discount operators pressuring the prices downwards. In the case of the Danish mobile market, the average minute of use price of the incumbent has been estimated at DKK 1.84 [3] (€0.25) whereas the minute price of CBB Mobil is DKK 0.69 (€0.09) indicating a potential value destruction of DKK 1.15 (€0.16) per minute equal to a revenue reduction at the level of 62.5%. If the average revenue per customer is reduced accordingly, it would equate a potential value destruction in excess of DKK 8 billion (approximately € 1 billion) on the Danish market alone. As this market is only a fraction of the international market, these assumptions would result in a potential revenue loss based on 2005 figures on the Western European market in excess of € 75 billion. Measured in terms of customers, Western Europe only accounts for less than 25 % of world market.

This must worry the management of the former monopoly who are facing growing pressure from the discount operators. As with the airline industry, the consumption of mobile telephony increases but at a speed which cannot counterbalance the value destruction posed by the much lower minute charges. Therefore the discount mobile operators are not only carving out a piece of the market, creating value for themselves, but are simultaneously destroying the value of their competitors.

Most people today are familiar with decreasing airfares and the lower minute charges for mobile telephony but how does one measure potential value destruction in the grocery retail sector? The answer to this is less straightforward as no clear cut calculations can be made on, e.g. the average price of sugar per kilo and the total metric tons sold in a given period through retail outlets. In general, however, it is agreed that the discount grocery retailers' use of private labels lowers the costs of which approximately 20 % is then passed on to the customer. The potential value destruction a reduction of 20 % would entail for this industry is at the level of approximately € 176 billion in Europe.

This not only puts pressure on the competing retail outlets but also on the manufacturers of branded products such as Heinz, Hellmans, Gillette and Kelloggs as these companies will have to match the price/quality ratio of private label products or spend large amounts on traditional advertising.

When taking value destruction to the extreme one would have to offer a product completely free of charge, which is exactly what Skype did, and still does, by providing downloadable software facilitating free telephony over the Internet. Should this mode of telephony become the standard across the globe we would see a value destruction equivalent of the entire global fixed line telephony revenues stemming from minute of use.

Given this, the potential value destruction stemming from the introduction of a discount strategy is unstoppable once the disruption commences as most customers would not be willing to revert to paying more for the same or less.

A disruptive strategy, once released into the business world, could have far reaching consequences for the players already competing. In a worst case scenario it could lead to bankruptcies, as we have witnessed in the airline industry with Sabena airlines falling prey to the disruptive nature of the discount strategy and the value destruction that followed in its wake.

The discussion above provides some perspective on the potential value destruction that discount products and disruptive strategies can lead to. The following will seek to explore the nature of a discount product or service and how this compares to the more traditional product.

Lean and unbundled nature of the discount product

Many conventional products have undergone a process of bundling with either peripheral services or with other products in order to create stronger ties between the customer and the company.

Bundling within a product done by offering a core product with peripheral services included creates a package for the consumer consisting of the core product, e.g. the air travel from point A to B, and peripheral services such as onboard meals and free coffee. Such bundles cannot be unbundled by the customer and have, in many cases, been perceived as a necessary evil. How many of us can say that we have never been dissatisfied with the food served onboard an aircraft and wondered why we had to pay for it?

A different type of bundling exists between different products which are bundled and sold at a discount but where the customer actually has a choice of unbundling them. Examples of such bundles are travel package deals covering flight and hotel, PC systems sold with Microsoft software or peripherals such as printers and cars sold with insurance.

These two types of bundling are illustrated in Figure 8.2, showing bundling within products on the vertical axis and bundling between products displayed on the horizontal axis. An increasing amount of both types of bundling, and perhaps even a combination of the two, will lead to less transparency, as we shall see later in this chapter.

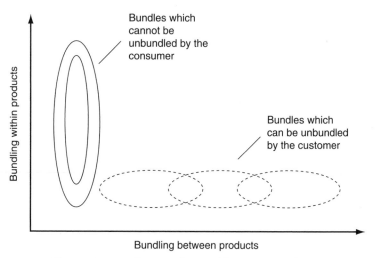

Figure 8.2 Bundling within and between products

Common to both types of bundling is the aim of creating stronger ties and maximizing the revenue potential, but where bundling between products still leaves room for choice, bundling within products does not. The latter type of bundling is part of the strategy SAS pursued successfully during the 80's by introducing the Euro Class segmentation, also introduced later by most other airlines. This class of passengers did not just buy transportation from point A to B but simultaneously purchased a host of peripheral services on top of transportation as a package.

Discount strategy takes a completely opposite approach by eliminating all peripheral services, which may be bundled into a product, and instead offers the core product or service. In addition to this, the product features, such as packaging and design, are equally reduced in order to pass on cost savings to the customer and raise the price/quality ratio of the actual product offering.

The product offered by low fare airlines is therefore characterized by including the travel only and no peripheral services such as free coffee, food or assigned seats. You do not even get a ticket when traveling with, e.g. Ryanair or EasyJet but instead quote a reference number at check-in. In conjunction with this lean and unbundled product philosophy, bonus schemes are non-existent, underlining that focus is on transaction based marketing where no special gimmicks are used to establish long-lasting customer relations. Any realized customer loyalty is a function of the superior price/quality ratio that the discount product offers.

Similarly, the mobile telephony product offered by CBB Mobil is concerned with minutes of telephony only and is stripped of all peripheral services or bundles such as a monthly subscription fee bundled with a subsidized and cheap handset or printed bills sent out every quarter as an added and bundled service. The product is simple and easy to understand with no hidden bundles or services as the customers buy minutes at a very low rate and nothing else. In terms of the grocery retail industry and Lidl, it is not so much the actual products but the experience of shopping at a Lidl outlet, which is characterized by an unbundled nature and simplicity. As such, no loyalty cards or discount cards exist and the articles held are displayed on pallets so the customer does not pay indirectly for the costs associated with exclusive displays or additional employees. There are no free samples or demonstrations of a particular brand and you will never find a Lidl outlet on the high street as this would increase the costs and this would have to be passed on to the customer. When you shop at Lidl you can find a limited assortment of articles that are cheap, of equal or superior quality to the competition, and you are not made to pay for the location or the costs associated with arranging the products neatly.

One analogy which can be used to frame the idea behind unbundling products and offering a simple, lean and transparent discount product would be to ask the following question:

Why buy a haystack when in fact you only need a needle.

Having this question in mind, the unbundled nature of the discount product makes perfect sense as some customers may not wish to be served a hot meal during flight, have an extra coat of paint on a new car, receive a printed telephone bill once every quarter, pay extra for having groceries arranged on shelves or have the previous version of a computer game bundled with the purchase of a PC system.

Viewing the bundling issue from a theoretical perspective, a U-turn is being performed, away from the predominant trend of the 80's where strategists embraced the additional refinement of Porter's differentiation strategy distinguishing between core services and peripheral services. After a period of increasingly larger and more complex bundles, the discount companies introduced a simple product focusing on the core and actual product resulting in the difference displayed in Figure 8.3.

In addition to focusing on the core product in an unbundled world, the discount product also focuses on a more narrow set of parameters surrounding the core product. For the discount carriers this involved abandoning the printed ticket, the pre-assigned seats, the use of sales agents and instead concentrating on areas which really mattered to the

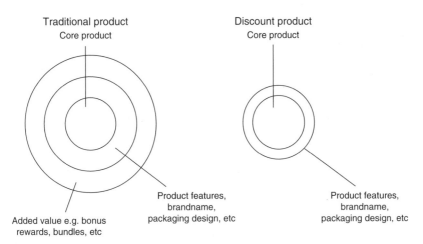

Figure 8.3 Levels of traditional and discount products

customer: on time performance, safety and price. For CBB and mobile telephony, the quarterly printed bill was substituted by online real-time billing. Discount grocery retailers such as Lidl turned their focus away from offering a wide variety of products to only offering those products with the highest turnover and displaying them in a bulk fashion. These initiatives are all of paramount importance in achieving the essence of a discount product, which has a higher or similar quality at lower cost in a simple and unbundled fashion.

In terms of traditional marketing theory, product differentiation is thought of as a prerequisite for branding. Four of the main categories given for differentiation are said to be the ability to differentiate the actual product, the design, the packaging and the services, as illustrated in Figure 8.4 [4].

When viewing the opportunities for differentiating on the actual product, traditional theory list areas such as *form,*

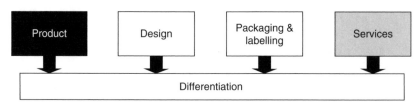

Figure 8.4   Areas for differentiation, based on Kotler

features, performance quality, durability, reliability and *reparability* as being of key importance.

Of these, *performance quality* serves as a major positioning tool as it has a direct impact on performance and this is where the focus of the discount product lies in offering similar or superior product quality at a lower price. Product performance is naturally closely linked to the *durability, repairability* and *reliability*, which is exemplified by the fact that, e.g. Ryanair has managed to outperform the competition in terms of on-time arrivals, an indicator of reliability, leading to a perception that its product performance is superior to that of rival companies.

Features, form and design are said to consist of those that are added on top of the core functionality of a core product to further differentiate the product and the actual look and feel of product. Examples of this in a traditional sense would be mobile handsets which have built-in cameras as added product features and removable covers creating a personalized product style or form.

The discount philosophy, or approach, in terms of these parameters is to remove those that are not essential for the quality of the core product thus moving in an opposite direction to what traditional marketing theory preaches. This stripped product version however, creates a strong differentiation when combined with, e.g. the discount price given the perceived superior offering in terms of core product.

Turning our attention to *packaging* and *labeling*, these may be hard to pinpoint when discussing services rather than tangible products. Referring to the packaging of a mobile telephony service or an airline travel service may therefore seem somewhat odd as these are not marketed in a specific container as is the case with grocery products such as milk. However, if we consider the environment from where, e.g. airline and mobile telephony services are purchased as a container for the product, packaging becomes of interest due to the differences between a discount and a traditional offer.

In the late 1990's the purchase of an airline ticket was done through sales agents whom you either contacted by phone or visited at their premises and as such the packaging for airline services consisted of personal contact. This approach was changed by the introduction of online booking via the Internet, which circumvented sales agents lowering costs and established a new form of packaging pioneered by the discount airlines. CBB Mobil used a similar approach for selling mobile telephony where the product was offered through the company website as a pre-paid service, also reducing costs. In line with the lean and unbundled nature of the product itself, the packaging was also stripped of unnecessary features resulting in an actual product, including core product and product features, which was much simpler and easier to understand.

The case of Lidl is more aligned with traditional thinking in terms of packaging but the lay-out of the store, which is said to represent the packaging of the outlet itself, was equally stripped of unnecessary features leading to broad aisles and products displayed on pallets.

When viewing packaging as such, discount strategy and the cases of Ryanair, CBB Mobil and Lidl encompass a lean packaging approach in line with the core product and product features emphasizing simplicity in its offering.

Simplicity is therefore also the key to how these companies have labelled their products as a no-nonsense, straight-forward and superior service or product in terms of price/quality. On the basis of this one could question the perceived level of service as many traditional services, such as finding suitable flight schedules, keep track of your mobile telephony bill and unwrapping a pound of sugar from a pallet, is now left for the consumer to perform. As we shall demonstrate below this ability to perform a 'self-service' has in fact had a positive effect in the market.

Self-service an important ingredient

It is commonly agreed upon in traditional marketing literature that services take on four different characteristics, which must be considered in any marketing scheme. These four characteristics cover the *intangibility, inseparability, variability* and *perishability*, as shown in Figure 8.5 [5].

Those areas, key to the discount strategy, revolve mainly around the aspects of *inseparability* and *variability*. It is

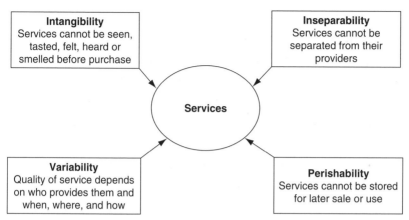

Figure 8.5 Characteristics of a service. Kotler, Philip, Armstrong, Gary, Principles of Marketing and Student DVD PKG, 10th Edition, © 2004. Adapted by permission of Pearson Education, Inc., Upper Saddle River, NJ

within these two areas that discount strategy deploys significantly different tactics that challenge conventional thinking.

The *inseparability* and *variability* of the services are highly dependant on who or what provides that surrounding service. In terms of travel agents, it would be the employee who you would speak to, or wait to speak to, and for mobile telephony it would be the customer representative, while at a retail outlet it would be the sales personnel. The employee or travel agent is therefore part of the service and as such the quality of that particular service may vary depending on the individual providing it, where it is provided and how. Now bearing in mind the statement of Richard Normann commenting on service, 'it takes 12 successes to make up for a single failure', the potential variability of the service could become fatal, so why not have the customers perform their own service.

This is exactly what the discount companies in all three cases have done. Ryanair have made booking available online where you can also search the flight schedules and assemble your own itinerary without being put on hold or having to browse through a never-ending menu of options, via your touchtone telephone. In addition to this, pre-assigned seats have been abolished so that you do not have to spend excessive amounts of time trying to find, e.g. seat E4, which decreases boarding time, achieving a perception of greater efficiency. In-flight amenities such as free coffee and meals are also non-existent, enabling the customer to bring his or her own favorite kind of coffee or tea and food or purchase something onboard if something on the menu appears interesting.

CBB Mobil has made refueling accounts and real-time billing information available online, which allows the user to keep track of consumption at any point during the day. This again can be performed without having to wait for the next printed bill or phoning the customer service representative who would then take your credit card details and refuel your account.

In the case of Lidl, the customer will pick the desired groceries off pallets which are loaded with the item in question, the aisles are broad and the stores are arranged to provide an easy overview of where articles are kept. This all simplifies the shopping experience and reduces the time spent in the store, while still buying in bulk. The majority of modern grocery shoppers are more than willing to perform the service of unwrapping the pallet given the lower price and the easier accessibility of the Lidl store.

Such self-service has increased the perception of the service level in general as you are given more flexibility to find and book your flight, refuel and view your telephony account details, greater accessibility in terms of finding your groceries at Lidl, and are always able to connect to the websites of Ryanair and CBB Mobil.

In terms of *inseparability*, the area of self-service is therefore viewed as a positive initiative from the provider rather than a burden on the customer. The variability of the service is in the hands of the one receiving the service and as such always on a par with what is desired.

This does not only lead to a perceived higher service but also a lower cost base for the discount operators who can pass these savings on to the customer, further increasing the price/quality ratio.

This approach also impacts upon the *perishability* of a service as in a traditional setting the required number of service employees must be on hand at all times regardless of whether or not you have customers to serve. With self-service, the downside of service *perishability* is avoided given that the customer performs his or her own service eliminating the need for excessive manpower, which, however, must be replaced with reliable processes.

Self-service is, as such, an integral part of the discount offering, not only for lower costs but also as a means to differentiate the offering from that of traditional competitors. The perceived higher service this may lead to, combined with the unbundled and lean nature of the product, results in a clear and positive positioning of the discount product in the jungle of highly complex bundles of products and services, which may no longer cater for the actual needs of the customer.

The intangible nature of services is familiar to all and as such buyers look for 'signals' of quality. The key for a company, with regard to this, therefore becomes to ascertain what quality is. Is it the lengthy time spent on hold while telephoning your local travel agent or the endless combinations you have to press on your touchtone telephone in order to reach the appropriate customer service representative of your mobile provider to ask for your latest printed bill? Perhaps it is the shopping experience of multiple aisles and neatly arranged pyramids of cans from which you hardly dare to pick one?

Discount companies such as Ryanair, CBB and Lidl have removed the majority of these surrounding services and focused on what appears to matter the most to the customer. The on-time performance of an airline: 'Do I get there on time and does my baggage also arrive at the destination?'; the range and reliability of a mobile operator: 'Can I trust that my connection – and in practice my talk with another person – will not be cut midway through a conversation?'; and the availability and visibility of grocery articles: 'Where can I find the milk, butter, sugar and is there anything left?'

A discount product, as described above, must be emphasized by a low price. This, along with the lean nature and self-service, is a key component of the discount product because without an aggressive pricing strategy, the discount product would lose its perceived superior offering of a better price/quality ratio. The following will elaborate on how such an aggressive pricing strategy is pursued.

Aggressive pricing

In order for the discount product to be successful, the price must be among the lowest in the market, or at least perceived as such by the customer, while at the same time offering the same or higher quality. Figure 8.6 attempts to illustrate the simplicity and the focus of discount on fewer parameters compared to traditional offerings, which paired with a low price results in a core product (what is actually demanded by the customer) of perceived similar or higher quality.

The aggressive pricing which must follow this simplified product offering does however, not only encapsulate offering a price lower than the Establishment but also a price significantly lower and thus generate a perception among the public that existing prices are indeed far too high. Pricing the discount product in such a way is a direct attack on the competition, which raises questions as to the appropriate level of pricing among customers. The idea is to generate a perception

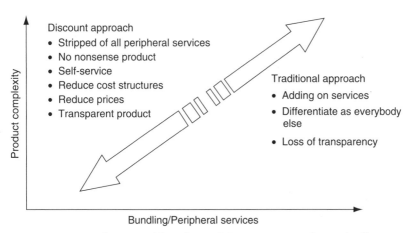

Figure 8.6 Complexity and bundling of discount vs. traditional offerings

among the public that they have been overcharged by the Establishment for a product, the actual core product, and that the discount companies have taken it upon themselves to rid the market of such an injustice.

Such a strategy will invariably also attract the attention of the media and lead to favorable publicity given that quality is at least on a par with a more expensive product. Ryanair is a prime example of how the media has aided them in their attacks on the Establishment by following closely, e.g. the lawsuit filed against Ryanair by BA as a result of their very provocative 'Gorilla' marketing. The aggressive pricing by Lidl on their assortment of grocery products likewise generates publicity, despite their management taking up a less public role as compared to Michael O'Leary of Ryanair, with journalists agreed upon the fact that prices will experience a reduction once Lidl enters a market. It has almost become an accepted fact in the grocery retail business that once Lidl comes to town, prices will drop.

Viewing the mobile telephony industry, and CBB, their aggressive pricing led them to be the first company on Danish soil to lower minute charges for mobile telephony to below the benchmark price of DKK 1.00 (€0.13), taking up a leading position early in the national price war.

Common to Ryanair, Lidl and CBB is that aggressive pricing, combined with the ability to offer equal or better quality, resonates in the media, the market and most importantly among customers. This scenario, as displayed in Figure 8.7, can be said to break the traditional curve of product performance over price.

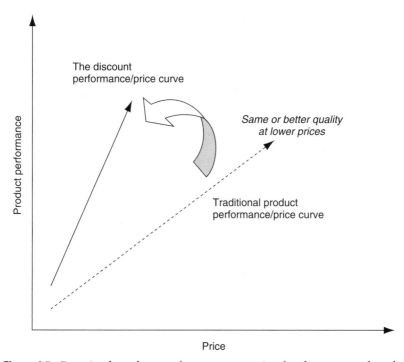

Figure 8.7 Perceived product performance vs. price for discount and traditional products

Aggressive pricing is instrumental in achieving a perception of a superior price/quality offering, and the importance of pursuing the position of the market price leader consistently can therefore not be overstated.

To illustrate the point, an online survey conducted by the International Air Transport Association (IATA) in 2003, asking what reasons passengers would identify as key to flying more often, found that price was a key reason, as shown in Figure 8.8 [6].

Based on the above we can deduce that the demand for air travel is indeed quite price elastic, which signals that the

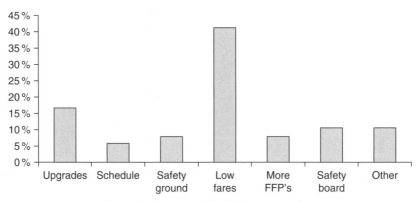

Figure 8.8 Reasons for flying more often

demand for low fare travel has been present all along but not catered for by any carrier prior to the introduction of the low fare airlines.

Similarly, the demand for cheap communication via mobile phone can be said to have been present, given the high amount of new users among the young in particular. This demand-driven nature of a product is a key element of a discount product in addition the lean and bundled nature, self-service and aggressive pricing.

Demand-driven products

Building upon our closing remarks in the previous section, the price elastic demand for air travel, communication and groceries leads to a situation where discount products are demand driven, creating a pull in the market. This has been somewhat overlooked by the traditional companies and exploited to a large degree by discount offerings.

This is highly evident within the airline industry, as illustrated in Figure 8.8 where price was given as the main reason to fly more often thus underlining the price elasticity of the air travel. This inclination to fly more often is not only relevant for current air travelers, but also for customers who used different modes of transportation previously or did not travel at all, as results from a survey conducted by NFO Infratest show (Figure 8.9):

As can be seen from Figure 8.9 nearly 30 % of people creating the new demand for low fare air travel did travel previously by other means of transport; indicating that low fare air travel is substituting for them. The introduction of low fares, lower mobile minute charges and discount groceries have therefore, aside from creating a new demand, substituted other products as people, who previously traveled by car or rail or used only fixed line telephony, were presented with a choice, offering a better performance at similar costs.

Another way to depict this and emphasize the demand-driven nature of these products can be depicted through indifference curves and the impact of a lower priced substitute product.

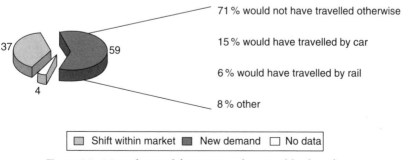

Figure 8.9 New demand for air travel created by low fares

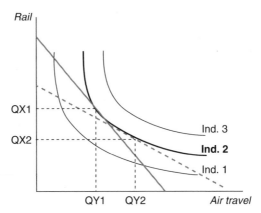

Figure 8.10 Substitution effect caused by price change

As illustrated in Figure 8.10 a price reduction on, e.g. air travel would alter the slope of the budget constraint, causing the customer to move away from rail travel.

Given this, the discount product is not only price elastic, which causes a greater demand at lower prices, but also a substitute for an existing product underlining the demand-driven nature and characteristics of the product. The characteristics of a lean, unbundled and simple product, offering a perceived high service which is in demand in the market, should result in value creation for the company that offers such a product.

Value creation

While causing value destruction for competitors, discount companies simultaneously create value for themselves, as described earlier in Chapter 2. This value stems from a clear focus on keeping costs low through re-inventing how the products are purchased and serviced. This should be done in such a way that the perception of the product is one of equal or better quality at lower prices.

The instrumental element in this is the lean and unbundled nature of the product, which allows for simple cost efficient processes and for involving the customer as a co-producer of the actual product. This reduces costs and allows for the discount product to be priced aggressively while at the same time differentiating the product from the traditional competition.

This, combined with the pursuit of a high turnover, where more seats are sold, more minutes are used and an increasing amount of groceries are purchased from the pallets of hard discounters, creates the value characteristic of Ryanair, CBB Mobil and Lidl.

Similarly, the examples given in Chapter 1 of IKEA, Skype and CostCo display similar characteristics with high volume sales at lower prices, leading to total value creation for the individual discount company.

As described above, the area of paramount importance when creating value through a discount product is the unbundled and simple product, which can be translated into a no-nonsense product. As such, there are no hidden, unwanted services or bundles within the product. Furthermore, the involvement of the customer as a co-producer cannot be underestimated as this serves a two-fold objective: lowering costs while increasing the perceived service level ultimately as part of a differentiation.

Back to basics

In this chapter the focus was on the key characteristics and emergence of the discount product compared with conventional products. Figure 8.11 provides a comparative overview of different strategic perspectives with regard to the role of the product and provides the key characteristics of an execution perspective.

Having created the product strategy, the next step in the development of the discount business case is to focus on branding, which is addressed in Chapter 9.

Key characteristics	Discount product	Conventional product	Execution tactics
Product focus	Value of the core product	Value of the peripheral services	Viz. that the discount core product is better and cheaper
Presentation style	Lean and unbundled	Complex and bundled	Focus on 'no nonsense'
Production of the product	Self-production or co-production	No self-service allowed	Allow the customer to self-control the product
Pricing	Aggressive (low) pricing	Pricing of an incumbent or monopolist	The discount product has to be *perceived* as the cheapest product
Product-customer dynamics	Demand pull	Product push	Create and exploit pull
Product value	Value creation and destruction	Value creation	The best interest of the customer

Figure 8.11 Comparative overview of different strategic product perspectives

9

A good brand is much more than a good brand

The growing importance of 'brandr'

In academic circles, there is a saying that brand equity is as important as the future cash flow of the firm. In the context of a discount strategy, however, a good brand might be even more important than that.

The term 'brand' comes from the Old Norse verb 'brandr' which meant 'to burn'. This relates to an ancient tradition of stamping livestock in order to claim ownership when animals roamed free on the range. Not only cattle, but also horses, sheep, pigs and other animals were subjected to branding. The branding of animals was customary at least as early as 2000 BC.

Cattle branded by a farmer with a good reputation would be more desirable than those of a farmer with a less favorable reputation. The employment of brands as choice guides for the purchaser was thus established from early times.

The phenomenon of the everyday use of the term 'brand' is a product of the industrial revolution, which created a mass market for consumer products and services. Many of today's highly recognizable brands are directly related to the emergence of mass market products (e.g. Singer, Coca-Cola, Kodak, Lego and American Express), initially on a local/national level and today often on an international/global scale.

Invariably, a proportion of the difference between the book value and the current stock share price value of a company is attributable to its brand equity value. In the case of the Coca-Cola Company, the 2005-ratio arrives at around 1:8 ($ 12.5 billion in book value as against $ 104 billion), giving scope for attributing perhaps 50 % of this differential to the brand value. Other well-known brands such as Pepsi, Cisco and Nike also show a significant difference between the book value and the market cap, as shown in Figure 9.1.

Indisputably, a lot has happened on the way from *brandr* to *brand*. From searing the flesh of an animal with a hot iron in order to produce a distinctive scar for ownership purposes to today's focus on the creation of *excess* ownership/shareholder value. In this chapter we shall address the importance of creating a good brand under a discount strategy. The starting

Billions of US$	Coca Cola	Pepsi	Cisco	Nike
Tangible assets	27.491	22.547	31.071	6.646
Liabilities	14.942	13.248	9.678	3.149
Book value	12.549	9.299	21.393	3.497
Market Cap	103.915	91.189	113.179	15.988
Book-to-market	8.3	9.8	5.3	5.6

Figure 9.1 Book-to-market ratio of selected companies

point is that it is much more important than 'just' creating traditional excess value in the transition from brandr to brand.

'You need to invest money in the establishment of a good brand'

Conventional wisdom tells the decision maker of today that it is both a necessary and a sufficient condition of success to invest in branding and the brand. It seems to be generally accepted among top management that branding efficiently and effectively is a costly affair. Needless to say, marketing bureaux, branding experts and management gurus strongly support this idea – including their own remuneration – and they all find a powerful justification in the fact that a good brand does add value. Consequently, there is a pay-off in many cases with the Coca-Cola experience as the case in point: if you are not a continuous high-spender in advertising, people will stop drinking Coca-Cola. If you are a continuous high-spender, people will continue buying your product and the goodwill of the company will increase extravagantly.

Industry statisticians support this mechanism diligently with weekly surveys on the levels of unaided and aided awareness. If the unaided awareness drops, you are on your way out of business, and the only way that you can increase awareness is to increase your media spending.

However, this conventional wisdom is all nonsense with a discount strategy. The philosophy is not that you need to invest heavily in out of pocket money in order to establish a good brand but rather that you need to increase the brand value every day at no cost.

It is hardly surprising that marketing bureaux, branding consultants, and management gurus never tell the story of how a brand is established, maintained and developed in a discount strategy, because there is almost no out of pocket spending. In other words, there is no remuneration for branding specialists and almost no media spending. Consequently, the lack of reward for the marketing bureaux means that they do not give any account of the success of discount businesses, and the sense of non-spending.

Establishing, maintaining and developing a discount brand has generally nothing to do with spending, but brand management is, regardless, a building block in a discount strategy for a number of very good reasons.

We cannot afford to spend

When strategizing discount, the conventional and unavoidable high media spending is reversed as: *We cannot afford to spend!* Thus, branding is everything else but media spending. Discount branding is isomorphy between branding and culture, between branding and vision, between branding and image. Not just a relation, but isomorphy.

Take the correspondence between the discount branding process and image when discussing media spending. A company pursuing a discount strategy is simply not able to create a discount brand if the company pursues high media spending, for obvious reasons. One is that most customers simply do not believe that a discount product is cheap if the company has high media spending. In the airline industry, the traditional flag-carriers continue to have high media spending (ads, sponsorship, marketing material, etc), but Ryanair has successfully done without most of the traditional promotional tools. Their customers do not get to know about the products through advertising but rather from friends and colleagues or from their own web-searches.

Concerning the anti-spending philosophy, the following example is illustrative of how discount companies work:

> One day the Marketing and Sales Director realizes that the press has been pressed too hard to provide 'free of charge' promotion for the company, and that consequently he needs to demonstrate at least some media spending (as journalists also believe in the conventional wisdom). Moreover, he has a message which suits the television media perfectly. He therefore somewhat reluctantly asks the Board for a budget increase (of a couple of millions) or alternative directions from the Board. This starts a discussion lasting at least two hours, and the Director actually succeeds in persuading the Board to grant him his request concerning TV ads, although at no expense ('as you know, we cannot afford high media spending – we told you that even before you undertook your assignment over a year ago . . . ').

> The Director leaves the boardroom somewhat confused but in a sense relieved because core values have been upheld. He starts thinking creatively and informs his team.

> He returns proudly to the Board 26 hours later, informing them that he will now proceed with TV ads without burdening the

budget. More precisely, he went through the list of companies who had filed for bankruptcy and compared it with the list of companies that had reserved time for TV ads. From one of these companies, he managed to obtain the desired television blocks for hardly any payment at all because the bankrupt company could not utilize the television blocks they had already paid for.

Such stories are typical of discount companies, and the story is not only remarkable because of the mitigation of cost but also in the context of the culture and the vision of a discount company. The story is also illuminating as regards the establishment of a brand identity and how the brand identity drives expectations [1].

Concerning the cultural aspect, discount companies tend to work far more systematically than conventional companies. One can even cast some doubt on whether conventional companies even deal with the cultural aspects of branding. Much attention is focused on the immaterial part of the branding, unrelated to the product and the production process, and a great deal of attention is paid to the statistical issues, not least the development of the share price.

Discount companies, on the contrary, tend to work with a very close link between the branding and the cultural aspects. This is shown in several ways:

1. During the recruitment process, the Marketing and Sales Director had been familiarized with the company's attitude towards spending. On a broader scale, it is seen at Ryanair, CBB Mobil and Lidl that discount brand goes hand-in-hand with the internal culture, as employees are

rewarded for displaying a creative attitude toward non-spending. *In the discount strategy a cultural character-istic is that the out of pocket expense for the branding process is kept way below the level realized in traditional branding thinking.*

2. An additional feature of discount companies is that the recruitment process and outcome is far different from that in traditional companies. For example, the wage level is generally lower, although expectations with regard to productivity are far higher. It is often seen at Ryanair, CBB Mobil and Lidl that skilled employees in customer care are recruited from competitors where they had a higher salary. Interviews show that, in particular, the younger elements felt stuck in the bureaucracies of incumbent organizations and wanted to be part of a young and efficient discount culture, where they could enjoy a 'go-go' discount culture eager to take on lazy competitors, the pizza and coke envi-ronment, the focus on technology, the company parties, and a life style where getting the job done even though it entails working long hours counts for more than the 'let's do it tomorrow' culture of the incumbent. *In a discount strategy, recruitment based on lower salaries and higher output demands is easy because of the discount culture's distinctive life style, which also imparts a freshness to the customers and the product.*

3. The simplicity and 'No Frills' character of the discount product also pervades the organizational culture where there is a very short ladder from top to bottom. Top management will often be in direct contact with shop floor employees as well as with customers. And employees will

have greater contact with management than is seen with competitors. Moreover, there is no time and room in the discount organization for a negative informal culture – the organization is simple and lean, and a true mirror of the product offered. *In the discount strategy, the 'No Frills' brand is already established in the organization and the underlying cultural processes – a true identification between the values of the brand and the values in the way the product and services are produced and delivered.*

4. Another internal cultural characteristic could be labelled 'Mr company personified'. Michael O'Leary, Pedersen and Schwarz all appear not only to have a strong external impact, but likewise to have a tremendous effect on internal cultural processes. Would Jack Welsh have had daily contact with the shop floor and individual customers at General Electric? Hardly. But Michael O'Leary is aware of every little detail and seems to fully understand its cultural impact. Mr Schwarz is likewise perceived as a strong and fully accepted leader. The internal popularity of the ultimate leader is often disregarded in larger organizations where, e.g. communication with external shareholders is given much higher priority (whereas the discount companies, with regard to the shareholders, seem to have more leanness than many other companies. Many discount companies actually started as privately owned companies of which a considerable proportion still function as such). Obviously, communication style – externally as well as internally – is very different as between O'Leary and Schwarz but the results seem to be pretty much the same. Similarly, other European discount brands are often personified as, e.g. with Virgin Express'

Richard Branson and easyJet's Stelios Heji-Ioannou. *In the discount strategy, simplicity is a winner with regard to the leadership; often the ultimate leader/owner personifies the company and this strengthens the internal cultural coherence considerably.*

In short, internal culture is a very important part of the branding process of a discount company. One can even go as far as saying that the cultural focus on competing, recruiting the young, leanness, innovative thinking, low salaries, and personification of the company make a very strong contribution to the discount brand.

David against Goliath

With regard to the company's vision, things are also far easier under a discount strategy than under alternative contingencies, where the vision is crafted and revised several times.

The vision of discount companies deals with simplicity, no frills, and good value for the customer. Basically, the vision of a discount strategy is to deliver the desired (or better) quality at surprisingly low prices.

Viewed from a branding perspective, such a vision makes it much easier to communicate and execute than is the case with the traditional company which has a complex product, an 'advanced' marketing mix and a go-to-market strategy with differentiated and bundled offerings.

This vision is top management's inspiration and aspiration for the company. In the case of discount, we are talking about an invention not yet comprehensively described so it can be a tool in the hands of the top management. That this can be described as an invention reflects the fact that a management process often starts from ground level in a business based on a discount strategy. This also means that the often critical issue of having the organization 'living the brand' seems more natural in the case of discount strategies. Discount becomes an embedded feature of the organizational culture and thus behavior.

In practice, this implies that top management can invent its own management principles, design the organization from scratch, depict the main stakeholders, and start the communication processes on its own terms. Essentially, these contingencies are the same whether you had failed initially with Porter's differentiator type of strategy and you then adopted a discount strategy, as with the Ryanair and CBB Mobil, or you were born more or less directly with a discount strategy, as in the case of Lidl.

In these and other cases, top management exploits the David against Goliath metaphor. In the case of Ryanair, Michael O'Leary in the beginning positioned Ryanair consistently in contrast to the flag carriers, notably British Airways and Aer Lingus. In the case of CBB Mobil, the CEO criticized the mobile incumbent continuously for its poor service, technical hindrances, lack of number portability, lock of SIM-cards, etc. And in the case of Lidl, their appearance in a new territory was well received as a fight against incumbents with prices that were too high and customer satisfaction that was too low.

Utilizing the David against Goliath metaphor is underpinned by creative remodelling of the stakeholders when pursuing a discount strategy. Conventionally, you would think of shareholders, the unions, the public regulatory agencies and interest groups as the prime stakeholders. However, none of these is the primary focus of attention when you have the discount price/quality vision.

Invariably, many traditional companies face a gap between vision and image. The image-vision gap [2] of such companies appears because of the ambitious visions of incumbents who already have gained a substantial foothold and enjoy a decent market share. This has to be 'defended' among the stakeholders in order to reduce this gap. Goliath has to continue, big is beautiful, and the show must go on.

The discount company is not a defender but a challenger. Some of the prime stakeholders are journalists and the media. They love challengers because they incur conflict and conflict is always interesting to cover, especially if the customers, the mass market, the young mother or the retired grumbler are impacted directly. Journalists will almost always be in favor of the challenging discount message.

Generally, journalists are keen on the disruptive nature of a discount strategy. When Michael O'Leary revealed that air travel with Ryanair would become free of charge at some stage, journalists were eager to interview the flag-carriers, where they either received a roaring silence or 'this is highly unrealistic'. Ryanair always tries to garner a lot of press coverage when they initiate a new destination. As Michael O'Leary has stated repeatedly:

> It is too expensive to get assistance from the marketing experts. Even in the few cases when we have to insert ads in the newspapers, we do everything ourselves in order to save money.

At CBB Mobil they also pursued a very close relationship with the press and managed to gain extremely good media coverage. At one stage, CBB Mobil introduced the new service of un-locking SIM-cards free of charge so that customers could shift more quickly to the company instead of having to stay with their former operator. Obviously, such a challenging move gained (as expected) a good deal of press coverage, including on prime time TV. The move was reported to be courageous and beneficial to customers – a perfect media story. After some weeks, industry pressure from vendors and distribution channels with mixed interests forced CBB Mobil to close down this service which again drew press coverage, including live prime time television.

Lidl is also getting good coverage although with less visible techniques. The press liked to write positively about Lidl as a challenger whose very low prices squeezed the margins out of the incumbents' business.

Moreover, we should not forget the fact that journalists are also customers themselves. They love cheap or free air travel, low mobile phone prices and more groceries for the same amount of money. In addition, journalists often lean towards the 'small and weak' in society, in this case the anti-incumbents.

The bottom line is that journalists give the well-functioning discount company a considerable amount of good coverage which makes ordinary marketing spending almost redundant. So-called political mass marketing through the press is probably a much more efficient marketing tool than advertising because success stories in the media are a more compelling tool for acquiring customers. One can argue that the crises of Ryanair and CBB Mobil left them with no alternative to political mass marketing. Not surprisingly, journalists are some of the foremost stakeholders in the discount companies.

Another type of stakeholder is the web-community, in particular chat-groups. Chat-groups are often difficult to identify because they are rarely organized. They may therefore be far more effective than is recognized in conventional theory where they hardly exist. General hear-say and rumour have always played a part in word of mouth recommendation of products and services but the emergence of the Internet has opened up exchange of customer experience through various chat rooms which exist in relation to most industries. As this is considered an important marketing tool at no out of pocket expense, discount companies take time to participate in chat rooms, providing facts and opinions. Chat rooms have therefore become a new stakeholder – a stakeholder in discount companies.

Consumer boards are also extremely important stakeholders. Consumer boards are usually founded on the philosophy that comparisons of products and services are for the benefit of the customers so that they can choose the cheapest solution at a given level of quality. Consumer boards therefore love discount products and services. They can even see the benefit of the mere comparisons in the sense that companies struggle to be ranked as the cheapest. However, only those discount companies with a disruptive business strategy can survive as the cheapest in the long run. Consequently, discount companies favor consumer board comparisons at least as much as the incumbents hate them. Not surprisingly, assistance to the consumer boards is part of the work program in a discount organization. Discount companies even try to broaden the types of comparisons. In recent years the picture has emerged with regard to consumer boards' statistics concerning customer complaints of customers filing far fewer complaints about discount products and services, with the incumbents having received many more justifiable complaints.

Obviously, employees and customers are also very important stakeholders in the discount strategy.

As already discussed, a clear vision of discount products and services is comprised of a challenging price/performance aspiration which ties employees and the customers together, sharing one and the same vision.

In a discount strategy the development of the brand deals also with the self-perception of the customer. 'This brand is me' is often recognized when participants in focus groups express their attitude towards discount brands like Ryanair, Lidl and CBB Mobil. The emotional and self-expressive benefits may become even stronger with successful discount brands than with established high-end brands like Jaguar and Harley Davidson [3].

The discount stakeholders	The conventional stakeholders
Journalists	Shareholders
Chat-groups	Unions
Consumer boards	Other interest groups
Employees	Public regulatory agencies
Consumers	
The general public	

Figure 9.2 Comparison of the foremost stakeholder

In fact the discount vision involves fewer gaps between the constituencies: who could be against much lower prices at the same or maybe an even better level of quality, except for the incumbents? However, as we have shown, the execution of top management's vision demands a careful identification of the prime stakeholders. As depicted in Figure 9.2, the general trend is that the successful execution of a discount strategy pays more attention to a number of stakeholders who are not the focus of attention in most conventional business cases.

As can also be seen in Figure 9.2, the general public becomes a friendly co-player in a discount strategy. This will be elaborated further when taking a closer look at the corporate image of the discount company.

The Gorilla image

Some years ago, the term 'discount' had mainly negative connotations. Discount products and services were automatically perceived as low prices = low quality. When buying at discount, customers tried to do it secretly for several reasons. Customer bought products which did not have the label of branded goods and services. Customers had to queue and wait for a longer time in order to purchase them. And the customer had to live with the possibility that the goods and services would have sold out when it was his or her turn. And how many executives have had a secretary order a monkey class flight ticket for them in order to save money and experienced the humiliation of walking though the business class cabin in order to arrive at a seat in the back next to the toilet?

But over the last five years, journalists in particular – but also business people – have completely turned the negative image of discount products and services around. Now, discount is generally characterized by:

1. The price is perceived as the lowest and there are no frills – *you do not risk being cheated.*

2. Your friends, your neighbours, the managing director and the press are buying the same goods as you – *now you almost want to be recognized as a 'discountee'.*

3. Usually, the discount product is better or at least at the same level of quality as all other products and services – *it is most likely that you even get a better product.*

4. You can order your flight ticket over the Internet, top up your mobile from the mobile terminal or over the Internet without queuing time, and the queues for discount groceries are shorter – *your ordering line is getting easier to manage, and your waiting time is shorter; it is 'discounted'.*

Given such improvements, discount is becoming increasingly a positive term and external stakeholders now associate a very positive image with discount companies.

As an image is the outside world's overall impression of a company, it is interesting to try to identify just one distinctive impression or expression of the discount company. It has become increasingly popular in the strategic management literature to characterize different schools and types of strategies by way of an animal [4]. However, discount strategies have not yet found a place in the literature. Among the animals left for metaphorical use, we suggest the Gorilla, alternatively the ferocious Bulldog or Wild Dog – as embodying the disruptive nature of a well executed discount strategy.

The Gorilla is one of the largest and most powerful of mammals. Its size and strong canine teeth usually protect it from attack. The male, however, will often stand upright and beat its breast with clenched fists, accompanying this with snarling barks and a deep guttural roar (if an intruder approaches but turns and runs away, the Gorilla may follow and kill it).

The Gorilla image associated with a discount company is very much a reflection of the real life Gorilla. The Gorilla image is based on a rethinking of the traditional marketing mix with an emphasis on place and positioning.

Given that the discount company has a very favorable offering to its customers – which definitely seems to be the case with Ryanair, CBB Mobil and Lidl – the marketing mix will inevitably focus on place and positioning. This is precisely where Gorilla marketing comes into the picture!

The CEO of the discount provider does not only defend his or her own territory but relies on the 'roar' as a means of attracting public attention and fear amongst competitors. Clearly, discount companies are dealing in some of the hostile elements of brand and branding which the media are not used to. This may be one of the reasons why Gorilla marketing is so effective. Another reason is, of course, that Gorilla marketing involves a great deal of conflict which is also interesting to the media.

This is most certainly true for the CEO of CBB Mobil and similar mobile virtual network operators like Easy Mobile, and it is also true for the 'silent roaring' Gorilla of Lidl. However, the world's foremost example of Gorilla marketing is probably Michael O'Leary at Ryanair. A careful analysis of his 'roaring' tells us that he exploits every opportunity to fight for his territorial, vested interests, and the following examples are provided in order to add flesh and blood to the Gorilla marketing dimension of a discount strategy:

A. Whenever there is an opportunity for it, claims, directed to the public authorities, that the incumbents are pricing their services predatorily, abusing their dominant position, and are trying to extend their significant market power into new business areas, are brought forward. This is illustrated by the significant difficulties faced by Ryanair when attempting to establish new routes.

B. At the specific location there will always be discussion about issues such as planning permission and other permissions, the cost of utilizing resources (collocation issues), cross-subsidizing of companies, etc. Despite various uphill struggles (in particular collocation issues at the Charleroi Airport next to Bruxelles), Ryanair has come across via the political mass communications machinery as a company fighting solely for the benefit of the ordinary customer, i.e. the general public.

C. Whenever there is an opportunity, the discount company will roar, because it makes sense in the image-building process. In the case of Michael O'Leary/Ryanair, he can contact journalists and get his roar across, facilitated by eager journalists (but if the CEOs of, e.g. British Airways, Lufthansa or Air France approached a journalist in a foreign country in Europe, the journalist would not recognize their names and thus from the outset be reluctant to write the story).

Continuing with Ryanair, the stakeholders firmly believe that Ryanair is the honest challenger and that the incumbents are just dragging their feet. The emotive part of Ryanair's image as being honest, a good deal for the customer, a challenger, an honest contender, etc. all combine to justify the roaring. Consequently, Gorilla marketing by Ryanair accelerates the vicious circle for the incumbents. The media coverage of Ryanair continues as the perpetual wheel, and the Gorilla survives splendidly with a frequent roar.

However, this is not specific to Ryanair. Stelios Heji-Ioannou from easyJet has learnt the same lessons. Moreover, Skype is an example of a discount and disruptive business case in which the Gorilla is not personified but is clearly present in the go-to-market strategy, with free of charge telecommunications as the silent roar.

Branding as a tool-kit in the discount strategy

Two business school professors Mary Jo Hatch and Majken Schulz have designed a tool kit for the corporate branding of a generic firm [5] with the main message that a number of elements have to be aligned. In the case of the discount strategy, this model can be further developed in a less generic way to reflect the specific modality of the discount focused company.

All of the three gaps identified in Figure 9.3 are important to address when it comes to the execution of a discount business case.

As a starting point there is the *vision-culture gap* which is seen in most organizations and may be grave, in particular in public institutions, semi State organizations, and in big private bureaucracies. In the execution of a discount business strategy, this potential gap is overcome by way of the 'we-culture', focus on the business concept and 100 % acceptance of the same, and almost invisible borderlines between top management and employees.

The second gap is the *culture-image gap* which is a particular problem for many traditional or incumbent companies. In the successful execution of a discount business strategy, this gap does not exist because of the identification and isomorphism between employees and stakeholders. The employees also take part in the chat room promotion of the discount product, accelerate the word-of-mouth effect, and value

Who are your stakeholders?

What do your stakeholders want from your company?

Are you communicating your vision to your stakeholders effectively?

Does your company practice the values it promotes?

Does your company's vision inspire all its subcultures?

Are your vision and culture differentiated from those of your competitors?

Vision-Culture Gap

Vision
(managers)

Culture
(employees)

Image
(stakeholders)

Image-Vision Gap

Culture-Image Gap

What image do stakeholders associate with your company?

In what ways do your employees and stakeholders interact?

Do your employees care what stakeholders think of the company?

Figure 9.3 The corporate branding tool kit of the discount company [2]. Reprinted by permission of Harvard Business Review, from Are the Strategic Stars Aligned for Your Corporate Brand by M.J. Hatch & M. Schultz. Copyright © 2001 by the Harvard Business School Publishing Corporation. All Rights Reserved

the stakeholders. Conversely, the stakeholders are generally enthusiastic about the discount product, including the employees.

Notwithstanding the fact that discount organizations overcome the culture-image gap, it is part of the communications strategy in a discount business to rely on this type of gap existing in competing organizations, which are often incumbents. Incumbents are characterized by dissatisfied stakeholders, no interaction between employees and stakeholders and no tradition of focusing on stakeholders, in particular the 'new' and important stakeholders (see Figure 9.2). The culture-image gap therefore paves the way for the use of what we have called the Gorilla effect.

The third gap is the *image-vision gap*. This type of gap also exposes severe problems for incumbents when they are challenged by discount operations. As the market for 'No Frills' products explodes, the value proposition of the incumbent is also under attack. How can you defend the traditional incumbent's focus on peripheral or augmental features that are priced excessively when there is a demand for better core products priced much, much lower? Arguably, the introduction of discount companies in a market increases the image-vision gap for the existing players.

Low prices as a new corporate social responsibility position

As part of conventional branding theory, companies have to make investments in Corporate Social Responsibility.

Corporate Social Responsibility (CSR) may be understood as the steps taken by a company, beyond the minimum requirements set by current legislation, in order to advance social and environmental values. From time to time, this process may involve a pinch of altruism.

CSR is nothing new and has existed for two hundred years, but it has recently accelerated. In 1994, only 20 % of the FTSE companies issued separate social or environmental reports on CSR issues. During 2004, this rose to more than 80 % with more companies stating that they were considering the matter [6].

It is easy for discount companies to deal with the CSR issue. CSR is built into the product and the service, which is delivered at the desired level of quality and at an unprecedented low price. Therefore, there is no room for a bad conscience, and no need to reward society by way of a monetary CSR kick-back or to outline in the annual report that excessive profits are mitigated by a number of CSR actions.

A good deal for the customer is sufficient justification under a discount strategy, and it would be entirely wrong to spend money on the justification of the company as such. According to the discount strategy, money is better spent on lowering the price for the customer. Low prices are the *raison d'être* of the discount company, and the need for symbolic justification by way of CSR initiatives, covering up the ways in which a company distorts the market mechanisms, simply does not exist [7].

Furthermore, the conventional focus on CSR is superseded in a discount business by the use of the social capital factor which will be explored more in detail in Chapter 10.

Brand extension and discount

It is debatable whether a company can achieve brand extension successfully. Virgin Express and easyJet are the prime examples, although it is probably too early to come to any definitive conclusions. Rumours have circulated that Ryanair, Lidl and CBB will extend their successful brand into other areas.

An example of brand extension is seen in the case where Stelios Haji-Ioannou teamed up with the medium-sized Scandinavian 'Telco' in order to create EasyMobile, thereby combining the discount mass market brand of easyJet with the telecom expertise of Telco. Success probably depends on the reaction of competing companies in the territories where EasyMobile intends to be present. After the first couple of months, EasyMobile had gained only around 10,000 customers in the lucrative mobile market of the UK.

However, the discount provider 'Yesss' (wholly-owned by One), in the far smaller territory of Austria, gained some 100,000 customers during the first three weeks of operation. This story is remarkable, with respect to branding, because the Yesss customers are not able to tell that Yesss is wholly-owned and run by One. They are completely separate brands, and One has even not made a brand endorsement of Yesss.

It is too early to draw any definitive conclusions, but it seems as if the lesson learned in the hypercompetitive market of mobile communications, with numerous established brands, is that brand extension risks amounting to overstretching for incumbent mobile operators. Therefore, we do not expect to see substantial brand extension by Ryanair, Lidl and CBB, and we would like to see a cautious approach to brand extension by successful discount companies.

The good brand

The lesson learned concerning the importance of branding of discount products and services, not to mention the company, is that branding is the *key*. The brand management of a discount company is therefore important in crafting and executing the discount strategy.

The story of the highly successful discount companies shows that brand management involves cultural aspects, the employees, the organization, the vision of the top management and the stakeholders. More than establishing a symbolic brand not linked to the organization, discount strategy operates with a go-go culture, a clear vision on price, and comprehensive Gorilla marketing, involving all internal resources and carefully selected external stakeholders.

The good brand is one and the same as the company as it is appreciated by the customers and lived by the employees. In branding, in the context of discount, a good brand is far more important than a good brand in the conventional sense.

10

The discount customer and social capital

The pivotal role of the customer in a discount strategy

The case of Skype is that of a company which has picked up 150,000 new customers per day based on a discount approach. It is possible to pick up an unprecedented number of customers in a discount business case, but is there a proper approach to customers?

The art of knowing and understanding your customers and using them as your primary channel of communication is therefore another critical building block of a winning discount strategy.

Not surprisingly, customer behavior and the relationship between the customer and the firm occupies a considerable part of the business management literature for good reasons.

Invariably, conventional theory argues for the high importance of the customer in almost any business case. The customer also plays an extremely important role in business cases built on discount strategy. Not surprisingly, the role of the customer and the interaction between the company and the customer vary widely in the approaches taken.

In the conventional theory the customers are the key. The customer consumes the products produced by the company. The customer is the object of the marketing done by the company. The tactics of the conventional company are, therefore, to *lock up* the customer by various means such as peripheral or augmented services included at no extra cost, individualized relationship marketing, loyalty programs, etc. Subsequently, the customer is retained for the next round, and churn is reduced or ultimately eliminated.

The perception and role of the customer under a discount strategy is entirely different. Some of these differences are listed in Figure 10.1 in order to put the profile of the discount customer into perspective. Later in the chapter we will deal with the key characteristics of the customer under the discount strategy.

When it comes to the execution of a discount strategy management has to be aware of the salient differences in the perception of the customers compared with the conventional approach. Under the ordinary management approach, customers are there just to pick up and number. Accordingly, it is the so-called 7Ps that are important in finding the right marketing mix (product, price, place, promotion,

View of the customer	Conventional approach	Discount approach
Object or subject?	Object	Mainly subject
Consumer or producer?	Consumer	Consumer and producer
Decision priority?	Peripheral services	Core product
Level playing field?	Stratification of customers	Equal treatment
Type of interaction?	Individualized relationship	Egalitarian transaction

Figure 10.1 Main differences in the perception of the customer

presence, people and processes). One might even go so far as to say that the customer is not directly part and parcel of the marketing mix in most conventional management processes. However, in the execution of a discount strategy, the role of the customer has to be elevated, based on in-depth studies of Ryanair, Lidl and CBB.

The new customer-centric approach is yet another factor which has paved the way for the success of the discount strategy. Dealing diligently with the customer is one of the cornerstones of the successful execution of a discount strategy.

Why are so many customers telling success stories about Ryanair? How can it be that the customers of Ryanair, Lidl and CBB are participating actively in chat rooms in order to promote their discount products? Why is it that the customers of those companies are happy to assist in the production process?

The answers to such questions are tied to the fact that the discount approach has invented a new type of customer, or rather has discovered that customers can participate actively in the execution of a discount strategy.

Customers as social capital

The question arises of what constitutes success of the role of customers of the companies in Chapters 4–6. However, it seems impossible to find a comprehensive theory within the management literature that applies adequately. This is precisely the reason for laying out the elements in the execution of a discount strategy.

Surprisingly, a compelling and inspiring approach to the role played by discount customers was found outside the traditional scope of business management literature.

Social capital and the discount customers – the X factor

In his attempt to explain why there is such a great difference in wealth and financial strength between Northern and Southern Italy, Putnam [1] concludes that individual trust (the single person), arising from interactions within voluntary organizations, spills over into public trust (trust among many people). The underlying rationale for the wealth in Northern Italy is, according to Putnam, that participation in voluntary organizations, such as a sports club, the Salvation Army, or advisory boards, creates a level of trust that eliminates transaction costs. Being a member of a tennis club, would you then cheat a fellow member colleague in a business matter, even if there was no contractual business agreement? Or would you break a contract with a fellow member of the Salvation Army, even if you could benefit from it financially? 'Hardly', would probably be the answer.

The importance of trust has paved the way for the so-called social capital approach, together with Coleman's focus on the ability to cooperate [2], thereby stressing the importance of trust among people at a general level.

In economic theory, a successful outcome is often explained by the input of capital factors, production factors and human factors. Add to this the management factor, utilization of core competencies or innovative factors from the management literature and you may still not have explained a successful outcome at the macro and lower levels.

Social capital is, so to speak, the residual factor, which often works at a subconscious level, because managers are not used to working with the social, capital factor.

In a discount strategy, social capital has become a very important factor indeed, because conventional strategy and management theory is unaware of the social, capital factor. Consequently, discount strategists are able to catch the conventional strategists by surprise, 'simply' because of the general lack of awareness of the importance of the means of measurement within the social capital approach. In a sense, the important customer tactic drawn from the social capital approach is the X factor of the customer's role in the discount strategy.

The social factor in the discount strategy

As was seen in Chapter 9, branding, or 'brandr', dates back to the transition to an agricultural society. The same is the case with social capital. Trust and confidence emerged with agricultural trade when farmers began to produce more than they could consume. Subsequently, they began trading with their agricultural surplus. Without adequate monetary systems, a strong legislative culture or appropriate enforcement mechanisms they had to rely on mutual trust and confidence with their 'customers'.

In industrially developed countries in particular, we have developed an adequate infrastructure and yet there are still very high transaction costs in the buyer-seller relationship. Social capital has thus become a production factor in conjunction with capital factors, human factors and physical factors. Obviously, social capital is by far the most neglected production factor.

Social capital develops over time from individual trust to public trust and may also include organizational and institutional trust.

While the flag carriers were continuing to develop more and more sophisticated customer terms and tickets through retailers, seating descriptions, advanced loyalty programs, etc., Ryanair developed the electronic ticket and the 'No Frills' product, thereby relying on the trust factor. Lidl and CBB did the same with their 'No Frills' offerings, thereby lowering transaction costs considerably. But why is social capital so important, and does social capital have any bearing on business strategy?

At the macro level it seems as if the notion of social capital has become recognized as growing in importance day by day. At a high level of general and/or institutional trust, considerable transaction costs are saved. Saving transaction costs adds substantially greater benefit for both the company and the customers.

However, social capital is equally important when it comes to the crafting and execution of the discount strategy. This can be illustrated in several ways.

First of all, a discount strategy is very much concerned with the build up of as much public and institutional trust as possible. In the case of Ryanair, this has been achieved by the numerous positive statements from customers, from the high frequency of repeat purchases of tickets and by an aggressive 'we'-culture. However, the strong demand pull is based on the high degree of trust and the correspondence between the words and deeds of Ryanair. Not only does Ryanair market itself as the 'low fare' and 'reliable' airline, but the customers can also see that the airline performs well with regard to price. Furthermore, the level of punctuality is extremely high.

Just imagine how much trust and confidence customers attach to Ryanair when, from time to time, Ryanair hands out millions of free airline tickets and still adheres to high standards of punctuality! And this goes hand in hand with the usual one-class seating compared with the hierarchy of reserved seats at the flag-carriers.

In the case of CBB and Lidl, there is also a great deal of hear-say among the customers whereby a strong recommendation is established. The opening hours, the 'No Frills' approach and the high scores at consumer boards add to the customers' perception of a discount provider having decoded the oxymoron (the conventional forced choice between high quality and low price).

The discount provider gives the customer 'a bigger bang for the buck', and the level of trust and confidence increases – the social capital factor begins to work. However, this is just the starting point as to how the prudent business manager executes a discount strategy based on the social capital factor.

Add to this the word-of-mouth effect (WOM) [3]. Not only has the WOM-effect generated an impact on the level of 80 % on every purchasing decision, but WOM also helps constitute a social coherence in and around the discount company with sentiments like 'we belong to the same herd', 'we share the same feelings and we have the same style' and 'we and the company are one and the same'. Essentially, the discount strategy does not deal with customer loyalty which has been the expectation of a conventional relationship marketing approach, but much more with customers' *identification* with the company and vice versa. Consequently, there is an isomorphic relationship between the values of the customers and the values of the company.

Generally, the WOM-effect appears to be somewhat overlooked by managers. This fallacy is probably rooted in the fact that much attention regarding the WOM-effect has been focused on event-driven organizations such as nightclubs, restaurants, sports clubs, amusement parks, theatres, festivals, etc. The traditional manager in the airline, mobile, grocery retail and almost all other industries has been satisfied, if the customers are satisfied.

However, our experience with the airline, mobile and grocery retail industries tells us that customer satisfaction does not lead to WOM per se. Something extra is needed. That extra could be a WOW-effect in terms of product offering or a company allowing the customer to be part of the creation of the product, maintaining control over the offering and consumption, and allowing for an individualized fulfilment of the customer's needs. Without a strong and company specific WOW-effect, a WOM-effect cannot be expected. The discount customer behaves emotionally and to some extent rationally at the same time. The discount customer is above all a *social* customer.

Social capital and egalitarianism

In addition to some of the values addressed above, focus should be turned towards *egalitarianism* as one of the core values of the prudent company pursuing a discount strategy. Uslaner – one of the advocates of social capital – distinguishes between social and economic egalitarianism [4].

Social egalitarianism underscores the importance of equal treatment of all people. Given the value of seeing each other as social equals, people feel at ease with each other and will be more likely to trust and to form social bonds that promote cooperative endeavours.

In contrast to this, *economic egalitarianism* takes as its starting point the approach that if you believe that economic stratification is justifiable, you have no need to trust others, in particular not those below you.

Conventional companies are based on economic egalitarianism while discount companies are based on social egalitarianism (see Figure 10.2).

The essence of economic egalitarianism is that the different treatment of customers may be justified based on the notion of customers being different and having different needs. The flag-carriers' segmentation, different classes, and stratified peripheral services; the (grocery) retail stores' different credit ratings and differentiated communication to customers, and the incumbent mobile operators' widely different packages with segment-specific offerings are all prime examples of this view of customers.

Under social egalitarianism all customers are treated on an equal footing, and this is indeed the case with companies that execute a discount strategy, such as Ryanair, Lidl and CBB.

	Conventional approach	Discount approach
Level playing field	Stratification of customers: • Different 'classes' • Good and bad customers • Rewards for loyalty	Equal treatment: • Open for everybody • All customers are good customers • The customer can shop freely
Type of interaction	Individualized relationship: • More service than requested • Relationship marketing • Differences are justified • No need to trust others	Egalitarian transaction: • One size fits all discount customers • Transactional marketing • Equality is key • Individual, general and organizational trust
Constituent values	Economic egalitarianism	Social egalitarianism

Figure 10.2 Social versus economic egalitarianism

All customers can receive the same products at the same price, and there is no *a priori* classification of the customers. Consequently, no customer feels cheated and a very high level of trust is developed. This is galvanized by the transactional nature of relations between the discount company and its customers in that the customer has none of the usual incentives to stay loyal towards the company. There are no financial or other reward mechanisms for staying with Ryanair, Lidl or CBB.

As shall be seen later in this chapter, discount companies have a much more loyal customer base than the conventional incumbents and, consequently, a much lower level of churn.

The background to this success is that the practitioners of the discount strategy have attained a complete understanding of how the generally undiscovered social capital factor works in favor of a discount strategy. Treating customers equally with 'No Frills' is the key for the CEO of a discount strategy, simply because equality generates trust which, in turn, lowers transaction costs considerably whilst at the same time creating identification with the notion of a discount strategy.

The dismissal of relationship marketing

During the last decade, relationship marketing has been appraised and many good textbooks on the subject exist [5].

Basically, we distinguish between relationship marketing and transactional marketing.

The former is based on the notion that customers should be segmented (and *not* treated equally) and that marketing ploys are aimed at creating customer loyalty. A prime example is the so-called flight bonus program [6], which contains aspects of both segmentation and loyalty/retention.

In sharp contrast to the build up of the relationship-based segmentation of customers, a discount strategy is executed without such a kind of differentiation. Segmentation is considered to be a segregation of customers which is entirely unacceptable under a discount strategy, being based on customers being on an equal footing.

Furthermore, the traditional focus on loyalty and loyalty programs is counteracted in a discount strategy by communication based on a transactional view of the customers. The customers are free to 'vote with their feet', and the CEO of a discount strategy does not set up barriers in order to achieve the detention – i.e. over and above retention – of the customers.

In the execution of a discount strategy, the focus is on the *economies of transactions*. The 'No Frills' offering is sufficiently attractive to create a demand-pull effect, and the usual marketing exercise with the attempt to orchestrate a supply push is made redundant.

This is clearly illustrated in the cases of the companies cited:

- Traditional flag-carriers typically have flight bonus programs and communicate constantly with their customers in order not only to stress the relationship but also to retain or 'detain' them. In contrast, Ryanair has no flight bonus programs but 'just' a competitive 'No Frills' product. Communication with the customer is centred on the price/performance of each transaction, and the underlying cost calculation justifies that each transaction is viable.

- Many of the traditional grocery retail stores and hypermarkets have repeated advertisements, special (proprietary) credit card arrangements, loyalty bonuses, in-shop arrangements, customer-specific offerings, etc. In contrast, Lidl does not rely on relationship marketing but simply on its 'No Frills', 'best-buy' offerings.

- Traditional, incumbent mobile operators circulate customer magazines, offer loyalty benefits, develop advanced and complex product offerings, including special services and features hardly recognized and used by the customers, and bundle the products. The customer is to be regarded as a relationship customer. In contrast, CBB is marketing its 'No Frills' products in a transactional manner vis-à-vis the customer. The customer has no lock up period and is free to go.

Essentially, the discount manager has learned that relationship marketing is a waste of money and energy in more than one sense, partly because of the out of pocket spending, partly because traditional relationship marketing represents a wrong approach. Under a discount strategy it is much more efficient to communicate with the customer in a transactional manner.

Instead of overloading the customers with information and services that they never asked for, with the aim of ring fencing and detaining the customer, valuable customer identification is achieved at Ryanair, Lidl and CBB simply by focusing on successful transactions.

Fine words butter no parsnips for the discount customer.

Therefore, the discount strategist goes back to basics, rejects relation marketing and focuses closely on more traditional transaction-based relations with the customers, generating direct value for money for the company.

Psychology, culture and the discount strategy

The view on discount

As was emphasized in Chapter 8, the connotations of the word 'discount' have changed in the past decade. The negative connotations of the past have gone and have been replaced by a more positive attitude.

Our contention it that a diligently executed discount strategy has to target the customers' perception of 'discount' very directly. Invariably, at least some customers have to be convinced that discount is fine in the first place in order to generate a demand pull at a later stage.

Exploitation of the cognitive dissonance

The theory of cognitive dissonance [7] can illustrate the tactics that discount strategists take into account when executing a business case. In the triangle between (a) the customer, (b) the discount offering, and (c) the traditional (monopoly-like) product, you will see the worst case scenario of cognitive dissonance (see Figure 10.3).

In the execution of a discount strategy, Ryanair and other discount companies have always started with the perception of the customer. The customer needs to be attracted to the discount offering, because this generates a plus between the customer and the discount product (see Figure 10.4). As we saw in Chapter 8, this can be provided by way of chat groups, consumer boards, the press, etc. Furthermore, the 'No Frills' product, as seen in Chapter 8, helps generate positive feelings.

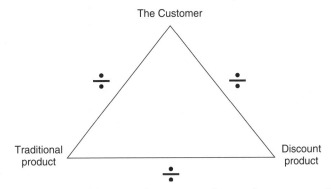

Figure 10.3 The unstable, initial situation facing first mover discount companies

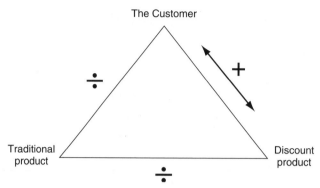

Figure 10.4 The 'stable' situation generated by first mover discount companies

Initially, the prudent discount company 'goes deep' with only a small peer group of customers. Once the discount offering is ready to go to the market, mobile discount companies, like CBB, Telmore, and Easy Mobile, kick off with only 5,000–10,000 customers in order to ensure fully satisfied customers. These 'peers' are constantly nursed and soon appear as ready opinion leaders for the next phase of taking up of customers. Strong opinion leaders pave the way for a demand pull in the market.

However, of equal importance are all the atrocities committed and accelerated between the discount customer and the traditional product. This is often by way of discount companies criticizing the incumbent with statements like:

- 'Monopoly products'

- 'Incumbent "service"'

- 'High price, low quality'

- 'No transparency of the product'

- 'Bureaucracy: Keine Hexerei, nur Bureaukratie'

- 'Old-fashioned leaders and greedy employees eating "caviar in the canteen"'.

Inevitably, this will foster awareness in the media which facilitates the generation of the 'minus' between the customer and the traditional product. Arguably, there is a knock on effect on the relationship between the traditional product and the discount product.

In the customers' perception, all of this creates a stable cognitive picture characterized by a positive attitude towards the discount offerings, whilst at the same time accelerating the negative attitude towards the traditional product and strengthening the negative relation between the traditional product and the discount offering (where a minus multiplied by another minus generates a plus!).

Life-style and satisfaction

It is interesting to see that the discount operation is usually focused very much on life style issues. To take an example, the initial mobile discount offerings are picked up very frequently by customers characterized by low income, youth, male, low to moderate spenders, etc. These are the early adopters and perhaps also the ideal stratification for a satisfactory low price-decent quality offering.

It appears from many customer surveys that the discount customers of successful companies, like Ryanair, Lidl and

CBB, are also the most satisfied customers, often with levels of satisfaction over and above 90 %, compared with an average of no more than half of this at the traditional incumbents.

Needless to say, satisfied customers are important, and, arguably, rely on a positive life-style perception of the product. Moreover, it is seen in many businesses that some customers even adopt a life-style approach to the promotion of the discount product that they are consuming themselves!

Price elasticity is also an issue in this context. Discount customers frequently buy discount because it enables them to see themselves as just a bit smarter and more intelligent than the customers at the incumbents, who are all paying too much for what is essentially the same product. In this sense, price awareness has grown rapidly with the success of discount companies.

The advent of the viral ambassador

We have already touched briefly upon key cognitive and psychological concepts from consumer behavior regarding the WOM-effect, peer pressure, the opinion leader concept, etc.

The WOM-effect is an extremely potent, inexpensive and often underestimated channel of communication. Moreover, the significance of the WOM channel increases exponentially during take off in discount business cases for several reasons.

One is that the level of end user confusion increases dramatically with the intervention of discount companies.

All the traditional, incumbent companies – such as flag-carriers, mobile incumbents and traditional grocery stores – retain their existing offerings when the discount company appears as the new kid on the block. Moreover, they tend to add new offerings in order to counteract the discount companies.

Another reason is that the discount company has its own offerings and that other discount companies appear with yet further types of offering.

In this context, WOM is the most reliable means of communication, and the word-of mouth channel impacts as much as 80 % on all purchase decisions. Where the WOM-effect stops, group pressure and group alignment start. This effect is strengthened by the pressure exerted in the chat rooms where discount offerings are often discussed.

Simple *honesty* is a critical concept here, which goes hand in hand with 'No Frills'. In the Internet world, the viral ambassadors have an easy job. Numerous ambassadors simply take their electronic address book and forward offerings from, e.g. Ryanair and CBB to all their contacts.

> I had no idea of a discount product before but one of my colleges told me in an email about this new offering with 'No Frills'. Wawoo – it is much cheaper and even a better deal for me because it precisely matches my need. I took my notebook immediately and sent SMS's with a recommendation to all my 76 friends and contacts to join the discount product immediately'.
>
> (from interviews with discount customers).

The successful execution of a discount strategy relies on what we can call the 'extended WOM-effect' in that the ambassador of discount also uses the Internet, chat rooms and SMS in order to promote voluntarily the discount offering.

So, the discount business case also implies the advent of the true viral ambassador.

The patronizing of customers

The rise and fall of patronizing

There are a number of anecdotes as to how the customer is commonly perceived as ignorant, and it is therefore important to look into what we have chosen to call the 'patronizing' of the customer.

As is usually the case, incumbents compete on yet more elaborate (and sometimes obscure), augmented or peripheral product features.

Thus, product offerings are growing increasingly inflated – this is especially relevant to industries where the product itself is somewhat commoditized and therefore must be differentiated on augmented features.

There is abundant evidence that demonstrates how the increasingly commoditized products, correlated with sophisticated marketing exercises, make less and less sense (see Sharp & Dawes, 2001) [8]:

The mainstream marketing reality is that brand choice is a trivial concern because, for consumers, the feature differences between competitive brands are not great. Whether it is Ford or Chrysler, Kodak or Fuji, either will usually do. Purchase preference certainly exists but it is often a function of salience (each buyer knows some brands better than others), habit ('this is the one we usually buy') and/or availability ('this one has my size'), rather than product differences between the brands.

Invariably, a mix with high price, poor real product differentiation, and a vast number of more or less useless peripheral services calls for a marketing communication exercise where the customer is patronized.

This appears, however, to be precisely the ticket to admission for the discount business case, because an increasing number of customers – in particular those with a predisposition for discount – reject being patronized.

Increasing brand promiscuity

Relationship marketing is an example of how incumbents think. According to our research, relationship marketing in a discount scenario is more dead than alive. At the very least, in the discount strategy scenario, relationship marketing programs (e.g. including various loyalty schemes, etc) are indifferent and only add to the patronizing of the consumer, whilst many customers feel alienated.

Relationship marketing is a means of obtaining a sustainable competitive advantage and the best way to retain or detain customers in the long run is the ability to develop *individualized* relationships with each customer seen from the company's point of view (which is, of course, quite different from the discount approach where the customer initiates the individualization).

Relationship marketing is designed to increase customer retention, because it makes good business sense to keep existing customers happy instead of devoting high levels of marketing effort to stem customer turnover, when every customer that leaves has to be replaced so that the company can merely stand still. Moreover, relationship marketing allows for a brand diversification, sub-branding, separate product branding, etc which leads eventually to an increased level of confusion and makes churn easier for the customer.

This may be illustrated by the churn levels in the mobile communications industry. The starting point here are the incumbents, many of which face churn levels around 50 % a year. Invariably, this is where relationship marketing, loyalty programs, peripheral services, etc, take off, whilst at the same time the patronizing of the customer begins. Interestingly, the churn levels of the discount providers have been much lower. From time to time it has been as low as 10 % on a yearly basis.

In traditional non-commodity advertising, price is often viewed as a credible representative of quality. When dealing with a commodity, this can obviously not be achieved, and the customer feels cheated or patronized by the incumbent players who constantly develop new price plans and packages, thereby increasing the customer's confusion.

Even the most well-planned relationship marketing programs may end up in increased confusion, once the former incumbents are challenged by the disruptiveness of discount companies delivering 'No Frills', whereas the incumbents have casual, occasional or fortuitous relations with their customers.

Arguably, this is the foremost task in the marketing tactics of a discount business – it must make the market leaders look arrogant, deceiving, promiscuous, and patronizing!

Simplicity prevails

The more incumbents pursue these costly strategies of differentiation, the more they enable simplicity and transparency in the product offering to appear as revolutionary and score points.

The relationship between the company and the buyer is strictly transaction-based – if industry conditions are favorable (many players are doing the opposite) as was the case in the airlines, telecommunications and grocery retail industries, it allows the discount operator to distinguish itself by being transaction-based (i.e. on simplicity and transparency).

In other words: the world and its customers search constantly for rationality. With other industry players clouding their messages and adding to end user confusion, a 'No Frills' discount product offering provides not only a lower price, but also allows the customer to increase the level of rationality in his or her purchase decision. This is a critical fact adding to simplicity and transparency and is in sharp contrast to the traditional trend to patronize the customer.

How to save costs and increase perceived quality?

It should not be underestimated that there are critical, yet positive, psychological effects in integrating the customer into the production process (the value chain). In Chapter 8 it was emphasized that self-service is an important component of the discount product.

At Lidl you have crates and boxes as opposed to neat displays. At CBB you log on and top up your account and settle all payment transactions yourself. Furthermore, you define your own service profile, and you can subscribe and unsubscribe to services electronically. At Ryanair you have online ticket purchasing, free seating, etc.

In addition to cost savings and increased quality, self-service or the customer elevated as co-producer also have positive psychological effects – there is no patronizing of the customer.

The main execution tactics

We have focused on the discount customer in this chapter. Figure 10.5 provides an overview of the main execution tactics that we have identified.

Discount approach	Execution tactics
The customer mainly as subject	*'We-culture also includes the customers help generate anti-patronizing*
Consumer and producer	*Self-service generates strong WOM-effect and vice versa*
Core product	*No frills*
Equal treatment	*'All on the same footing' creates trust*
Egalitarian transaction	*Transactional rather than relationship marketing*

Figure 10.5 The link between the discount approach and execution tactics

Evidently, the aim of the discount strategy is not just to be 'customer friendly', 'focused on the customer', 'providing additional services and extras to the customer', 'loyalty programs', or 'close relationship marketing', as in the traditional sense.

The prudent execution of a discount strategy turns supply push into demand pull, it turns demanding customers into co-producers, and it turns passive customers into viral ambassadors. The social capital factor then works efficiently and effectively in favor of the discount business case.

11

Finding the suitable technology

THE TECHNOLOGICAL ADVANCES OF THE 20TH CENTURY CAME about with tremendous speed and have changed the way human beings live and work. Computing power and networking capabilities have made the world a smaller place allowing for companies to reach new markets and reengineer their value and supply chains. Telephony has become wireless allowing for information to be shared in real time, no matter where an individual places a call from, leading to a more mobile workforce and less time wasted. Business managers across the globe are well aware of the benefits that come in the wake of technological innovation and may find it hard to imagine what the business world was like before mobile telephony, the personal computer, the PDA, the intranet, the extranet, the Internet and countless other innovations. But what about the technology of tomorrow?

When it comes to predicting the technology of tomorrow, many prominent people have in the past made predictions for the future, which in retrospect appear as far from target as they could be. The quotes below are among many but are perhaps the most illustrative in terms of how wrong business leaders can be:

I think there's a world market for maybe five computers

Thomas Watson, chairman of IBM, 1943

I have traveled the length and breadth of this country and talked with the best people, and I can assure that data processing is a fad that won't last out the year

Editor in charge of business books for Prentice Hall, 1957

There is no reason why anyone would want to have a computer in their home

Ken Olson, president, chairman and founder of Digital Equipment Corp, 1977

The fact that predicting the future is a risky game comes as no surprise to the majority of today's managers but the potential return of picking the technology of the future still tempts many to pursue a technology-based strategy.

Companies who have come out as winners based on such an initial strategy include Microsoft, Cisco Systems and Sony who are all considered global leaders within Internet working, computer processing and portable audio and video devices respectively.

However, putting all your energy and efforts into the 'wrong' technology can make even the most successful companies stumble and fall from grace into oblivion. One such company was Digital Equipment Corp, which in the early 80's was regarded as a top performer among companies and listed in the best selling management book *In Search of Excellence* as a company one should emulate for success [1].

Unfortunately the persistent focus on mainframe computers and the gamble on this technology led to Digital Equipment Corp missing the market opportunities stemming from personal computers bought for household use. Their technology-based strategy proved to be fatal.

The fact that technology in itself is not necessarily a recipe for success became further evident during the dot.com hysteria, which proclaimed that presence on the Internet was the single most important key to success. During the heydays of the dot.com boom, entrepreneurs and venture capitalists embraced the seemingly new rules of business, claiming that traditional business models and thinking were a thing of the past and would not survive in the years to come.

Initial Public Offerings (IPOs) were performed by companies with little more than a web site and a business plan. Despite the lack of actual revenue streams and few tangible assets many such companies managed to raise significant funds. One such example is given in the book *Good to Great* by Jim Collins, where an entrepreneur with no more than a web site and business plan managed to persuade investors to purchase 1.1 million stocks at a price between US$7 and US$9 [2]. Without any revenue streams, employees, customers or company this entrepreneur managed to raise in excess of

US$ 7 million based on the hysteria surrounding the Internet and the dot.coms at the time.

The events that unfolded in the later part of the year 2000 and the subsequent bursting of the bubble put a drastic end to many of these endeavors as well as signaling that traditional business thinking could not yet be entirely dismissed. It underlined the fact that the Internet, or any other technology, per se would not guarantee success but could and probably would if it was implemented as a part of a strategy rather than being the only strategy.

This point is emphasized in later management literature and in particular in the book *Good to Great* and the article 'What Really Works' [3]. The latter explains by way of the '4 + 2 model for business success' that a company must excel at the four primary management practices of *Strategy, Execution, Culture* and *Structure* and two of the four secondary practices *Talent, Innovation, Leadership* and *Mergers* and *Partnerships*.

The analysis made by Nohria et al. of approximately 200 companies and their experiences over a 10-year period showed that no relationship existed between the successful companies and any specific technology. The approach however, of implementing technology driven by the strategy and a clear judgment of whether the new technology enhances a business's performance in relation to the market, proved to be a better recipe for success.

As such success does not stem from the technology itself but the ability to identify the right technology and use it to execute the strategy.

Finding technology

Finding technology is not the real challenge in order to execute successfully. Ample technology solutions are at hand or may be developed easily. However, making the *right* technology decisions is yet another and much more difficult issue.

Technology decisions are important, because they have a considerable impact, not only on the production of the product and services, but also on the entire delivery system, including the logistics. The entire value chain of a company as well as the wider supply chain is to some extent determined through strategic choices. One example of this is Dell Computers who decided to eliminate the 'middle man' and deliver PCs directly to the customers, thus altering the traditional supply chain and leading to a new value chain. The decision to use the Internet as a sales channel was made on the back of their strategy to sell directly to the customers and as such fitted the strategy rather than being the strategy.

Simplifying the value chain, the supply chain and the entire delivery mechanism, in order to deliver better value to the customer, is at the essence of a discount strategy. The choices of technology implemented to support and successfully execute such a strategy must be driven by this.

When viewing the value chain of a discount company versus that of a more traditional company, the simple 'No Frills' discount product allows for a more lean and simple chain. This will impact not only upon the primary activities from Inbound Logistics to Service but also the support activities of the chain as less procurement, human resource management, firm infrastructure and technology development is required.

The value chain of a traditional company pursuing a diversification strategy, such as British Airways, will most likely include multiple products or product categories, bi-products and auxiliary services. This will lead to a more complex value chain, where all primary activities are geared towards different products, which in turn require a more complex structure of support functions.

To illustrate the point above, the example of a passenger flight between London and Frankfurt is used in Figure 11.1 which depicts a reduced value chain of a traditional passenger carrier in relation to such a scheduled flight.

In terms of technology, the multiple ticket classes in the example above may be marketed in various ways such as

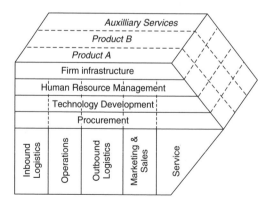

- Multiple ticket classes leading to products A & B
- Each product travels the value chain in its unique way
- As such two value chains are employed
- Each requiring product specific primary and support activities
- Resulting in a complex value chain, increasing the cost base

Figure 11.1 Value chain of a traditional airline company. Adapted with the permission of The Free Press, a Division of Simon & Schuster Adult Publishing Group, from Competitive Advantage: Creating and Sustaining Superior Performance by Michael E. Porter. Copyright © 1985, 1998 by Michael E. Porter. All Rights Reserved

through the Internet and sales agents, requiring potentially a more complex technological infrastructure. The delivery of the actual transportation from London to Frankfurt may be done using multiple types of airplanes, which again further complicates not only the operations but also the supporting activities. The various ticket classes may require different meals to be served onboard, impacting upon the inbound logistics, leading to an even more complex value chain. If additional products and services, such as lounge services and transfer to other flights, are added to the example above and multiplied by the average number of destinations of a traditional flag carrier, the complexities become large and demanding.

A discount strategy seeks to simplify the value proposition and also the value chain through the notion of a 'No Frills' product, as illustrated in Figure 11.2.

When adding on the 'self-service' nature of a discount offering, the value chain will go through a further compression

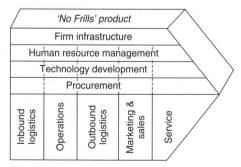

- One ticket class
- Leading to simplified value chain
- Impacting both primary and support functions
- Leaner cost base

Figure 11.2 Value chain of a discount airline company. Adapted with the permission of The Free Press, a Division of Simon & Schuster Adult Publishing Group, from Competitive Advantage: Creating and Sustaining Superior Performance by Michael E. Porter. Copyright © 1985, 1998 by Michael E. Porter. All Rights Reserved

horizontally due to the reduced amount of resources tied up in service delivery. This in turn also compresses the value chain vertically as fewer employees are needed thus reducing the costs of human resource management.

All in all, the simplified nature of a discount value chain should lead to a leaner structure allowing for simpler processes throughout the chain. This however, does not necessarily mean that discount companies are deploying second rate technology. It merely suggests that the technology necessary to support a discount strategy is focused more on a simple offering and supporting this offering rather than new emerging and all conquering technology.

The innovator's dilemma and the innovator's solution

To further illustrate the point that the latest technology isn't necessarily the right technology 'The Innovator's Dilemma', coined by Clayton Christensen, is used as an analogy. The dilemma arises when companies overshoot the technological innovation and thus what is actually needed in the market.

As seen in Figure 11.3, Clayton Christensen distinguishes between *sustaining innovations* which targets demanding high-end customers with better performance than what was previously available, and *disruptive innovations*.

The *disruptive innovations* do not intend to bring technologically advanced products to the market but 'are simpler, more

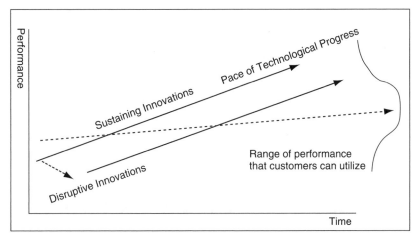

The Disruptive Innovation Model – Christensen, 2003, Harvard Business School

Figure 11.3 Clayton Christensen's model for disruptive innovation [4]. Reprinted by permission of Harvard Business Review, from The Innovative Solution: Creating and Sustaining Successful Growth by C.M. Christensen & M.E. Raynor. Copyright © 2003 by the Harvard Business School Publishing Corporation. All Rights Reserved

convenient, and less expensive products that appeal to new or less-demanding customers' [5].

Combining this with the fact that the discount value proposition finds its strength in the market of customers, who were previously over catered for, the discount companies may not need to rely on disruptive innovations.

They may not even need to keep up the pace of sustaining innovations, but instead align proven reliable technology with the strategy of delivering a 'No Frills' product offering superior perceived value.

Similar to the notion of overshooting the market, implementing the latest technology within the company may therefore not result in any competitive advantage. In fact, it may lead to the very opposite given a potentially higher risk associated with new and unproven technology.

The choice of technology must therefore support the lean nature of a discount strategy and the simplicity of such.

The choice of 'discount' technology

The companies from the three case examples all belong to widely different industries albeit with common characteristics: mature industries that have reinvented or innovated themselves many times over the past century, becoming fiercely competitive.

The airline industry has seen the range and size of planes grow through sustained innovation whereas the development and deployment of Concorde can be argued to have overshot the market. The telecommunications industry has gone from the ever improving speech quality of fixed network communications to low quality wireless communications, and the grocery retail industry has developed numerous store formats and adopted sophisticated technologies for, e.g. sales and store tracking, although the 'simple' discount chains take the lion's share of the market growth.

Despite the fact that Ryanair, CBB, and Lidl belong to widely different industries, there are striking similarities in how technology is chosen. All three companies' choice of technology supports the simplicity of the discount value proposition striving for 'as good or better at a significantly lower price' while allowing for growth, which is equally essential to the discount strategy.

The areas identified as common to all three cases in terms of technology concern the implementation, or use of, proven *'play safe'* technology, scalability, supporting simplicity and efficient back office systems. This leads to four characteristics common to the discount companies but pertaining to the underlining drivers of what a technology must contribute in order to execute the strategy.

Figure 11.4 lists these four common denominators and how they relate to the individual companies Ryanair, CBB and Lidl.

Though stated briefly in the figure above, a further description of the individual denominators is worth considering.

Ryanair, CBB, and Lidl	Common denominator
Ryanair deploys identical airplanes in their fleet. High turn rates. CBB relies on IN technology and Lidl operate the same store lay-out across Europe	*Proven, 'play safe' technology*
Ryanair uses Internet technology and plains that may be bought again, CBB uses on-line SIM-card production, and Lidl has fully described concepts to open up new retail Outlets	*Scalable technology*
Ryan goes for electronic ticketing, no seating reservation, etc., CBB gives the customer his/her own homepage and allows for real-time changes initiated by the customer, and Lidl pursues an easy access concept	*Technology suited for simplicity*
'No Frills', simple product supply, focus on volume and scalability (rather than differentiation), real time technology, etc., facilitates the back office systems	*Easy, 'simple' back office systems*

Figure 11.4 The common denominator of discount companies

Proven technology

When Ryanair decided to harmonize their fleet into consisting of only the Boeing 737, this presented a technically proven airplane with a good record, not to mention the cost savings associated with training and maintenance. By this Ryanair obtained high turnover rates. The online booking system Ryanair.com was not launched until 1999 and was done so on the back of strategic moves to reduce sales and distribution costs such as commission fees paid to travel agents.

CBB employed the Internet as more than a sales channel allowing for customers to view online account information in real time and manage their consumption through refueling online. This minimized the risks of multiple points of failure given its simple nature and its 'self-service'.

The store concept of Lidl has in itself proven to be a *'safe play'* and is used throughout Europe with every store displaying wide aisles, the same simple architecture and being situated for easy access. The simplicity of the building and the lay-out reduces the time required to set up new locations and for restocking, allowing for efficiencies.

Scalability

The long lifespan of a Boeing airplane and the number manu-factured, allowing for second hand purchasing, combined with the Internet as a sales channel provides the desired scala-bility. As an added bonus Ryanair purchased a large number of their 737s at bargain prices due to the recession in the industry.

Operating as a virtual network operator, CBB leases the network capacity of a third party supplier thus ensuring the proven nature and scalability of the delivery mechanism for the service of mobile telephone calls. The online SIM card production and outsourced distribution of the same can be scaled in line with growth without any significant investments.

Lidl's strategy of proven identical store concepts allows for rapid entrance into a market given the short amount of time required to make a store operational. The scalable nature of this is evidenced by the 301 stores Lidl has opened per year, on average, over the past 10 years.

Technology supporting the simple

Ryanair achieved simplicity through a harmonized fleet of airplanes, a single class and ticket-less flights with no allocated seating. This simplicity led to Ryanair becoming the industry leader in terms of time required to turn around an airplane. The simplicity of this fitted well with using the Internet as a distribution channel.

By providing their customers with access to a personalized homepage, the billing process of CBB has been simplified given the absence of any need for printed bills. In tandem with lowering the cost, customers also appreciate the simplicity of being just a click away from their account details.

Impact on back office system

Given the leaner nature of the value chain of a discount company, the reliance on proven and scalable technology, the requirements of the back office systems of a discount operation are less strenuous compared to those of a traditional competitor pursuing a diversification strategy.

This latter point is equal for all three companies leading to efficiency gains and higher productivity as not only less technology is needed to execute a discount strategy but also fewer employees.

These examples should all illustrate the paramount importance of choosing the right technology as opposed to the newest or most sophisticated. Only a technology which will support the lean objectives of a discount strategy, including its reluctance to spend excessively on technology, and thus act as just another cornerstone of a strategy as opposed to being the strategy, will succeed.

The examples above and their effect on a discount business are given in Figure 11.5.

As can be gathered from Figure 11.5 the choice of suitable technology has a considerable impact upon discount business. To illustrate the impact in more depth, technological effectiveness, efficiency and productivity will be elaborated further.

Common denominator	Effect on the discount business case
Proven, 'play safe' technology	Few points of failure
Scalable technology	No immediate capacity constraints
Technology suited for simplicity	Quicker sales process, high effectiveness
Easy, 'simple' back office systems	High efficiency and productivity

Figure 11.5 The technology impact on the discount business case

Technological effectiveness is straightforward, because it deals with the question of whether the technology chosen generates the desired outcome. As we have seen in the case of Ryanair, the standardization of the fleet combined with no pre-assigned seats led to faster turnaround times while reducing the costs of training and maintenance that are required when operating a fleet of various types. Similarly, CBB reduced their cost base through online account information while increasing the perceived level of service among their customers. The store lay-out of Lidl and the bulk manner in which goods are displayed allow for easy access and quicker restocking as well as a higher inventory turnover.

Technological efficiency is more difficult to assess as it deals with an overall assessment as to how the chosen technologies support the internal processes and procedures. Obviously, this is impossible to assess from an external perspective. However, based on the success of the discount companies, efficiency seems to be high, whereas the incumbents seem to struggle from time to time. One example is billing and administrative issues. A great deal of criticism has been generated by the fact that a number of the flag-carriers charge customers differently depending on which country they book their air-travel ticket in (cf. the simplicity and equality and subsequent administrative 'no nonsense' of Ryanair's uniform tariffs). Another example is recurrent billing issues at incumbent mobile operators (whereas the discount companies, with less complex billing technology, generally obtain a higher efficiency).

Technological productivity is a matter of comparing the input of production factors with the output in terms of economy. In terms of productivity there can be little doubt that the

Case	Productivity example	Estimated industry average
Ryanair	Load factor close of above 80% Profit margin of approximately 20%	Approx. 65% Approx. or below10%
CBB	One customer care employee per 15,000 subscribers (based on just 0.2 million subscriber)	One customer care employee per 5,000 subscribers (based on 1.5–2.0 million subscribers)
Lidl	Gross profit per m2 of € 955 Staff cost % of Sales of 5,6	€ 890 per m2 13,1% of sales

Figure 11.6 Increased productivity

discount companies score high given the significance of volume.

Concerning productivity, Ryanair, CBB and Lidl produce ample relevant evidence, as illustrated in Figure 11.6.

Figure 11.6 provides strong evidence that successful discount companies are utilizing technology in a diligent way in the production process. In this context it should also be taken into account that discount companies generally generate a much more satisfactory output vis-à-vis their customers:

- The price is considerably lower and the product offering often more attractive to the customers than traditional products from the incumbents.

- The customers are more satisfied and generally receive a better service from discount companies.

- The rate of complaints is lower.

The high productivity and perceived level of service has been achieved without making use of the most advanced technology but instead by aligning the technology to the discount strategy. By aligning the choice of technology with the discount strategy, the technology itself will be scrutinized and only the most cost effective technology will therefore be employed.

Technological exuberance avoided

When it comes to the execution of almost any business case, it appears to be conventional wisdom that you should invest heavily, and that there is a high pay-off on high-technology investments. This is tied into rhetoric such as 'we use the best-of-breed technology', 'we only deploy cutting-edge technology in our company', or even worse 'our R&D department is now two years ahead of any competitor with key technological features'.

Many CEOs are keen on the 'quick and dirty' implementation of new technology, which is understandable because there is what we label a technological exuberance, at work today. The CEO in charge of the execution of a discount business case is, however, more cautious and generally adheres to a restrictive view with regard to technology:

1. Technology is a good servant and should never become a dangerous master in the execution of the business case.

2. Proven technology is preferable – in most cases it is better to opt for technology that emerged two years ago than to opt for solutions which are expected to break through in two years' time.

3. In the case of a discount business, not only the offerings but also the underlying technology should be based on 'No Frills'.

4. Instead of technological complexity, solutions that imply simplicity are winners.

5. Technology has no justification in itself – technology has to help achieve substantial gains in productivity compared with the competitors.

Due to the above, the notion of technological exuberance can be rejected allowing for the focus to remain on technology which will support the execution of a discount strategy rather than vice versa.

This idea of technology being a tool to support a given strategy as opposed to the driving force is not unique to the discount business case. In *Good to Great*, Jim Collins also found clear evidence among the analysed companies that technology in itself would be no guarantee of success. Similarly, the work by Nohria et al. also revealed that no specific technology catapulted any of the companies, analysed in their study, to success.

What may be unique to the discount business case, however, is the conscious choice of proven and perhaps older technology, which is a luxury that can be afforded given a leaner and simpler value chain requiring less sophisticated technology. This relationship is illustrated in Figure 11.7 using an analogy with Clayton Christensen, where the

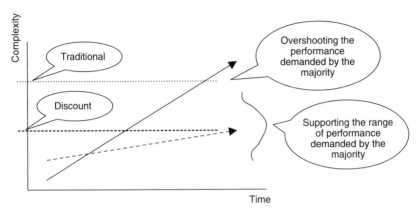

Figure 11.7 Simpler lean operations and the impact on technology choice. Reprinted by permission of Harvard Business Review, from The Innovative Solution: Creating and Sustaining Successful Growth by C.M. Christensen & M.E. Raynor. Copyright © 2003 by the Harvard Business School Publishing Corporation. All Rights Reserved

vertical axis represents increasing complexity of operations driven by a strategy to overshoot the performance demanded in the market leading to higher costs in terms of deployed technology, and the horizontal axis represents time.

Being one of four building blocks of a discount strategy, the choice of technology adopts the same 'No Frills' policy which is necessary in order to approach the market continually with an aggressive price strategy while seeking to maintain or raise the service.

Technology is a supporting building block, which, however, must be aligned with three other blocks and according to the design laid out in the strategy of pursuing discount. When technology is to be introduced in the discount business case, other elements are also affected as illustrated in Chapter 7. Therefore, the technology component has to be assessed according to a holistic view where technology is not just 'good' or 'bad'. Technology remains the servant of the discount strategy, not the master.

12

Value creation and value destruction

C RAFTING AND PURSUING A DISCOUNT STRATEGY IS BY NO means an easy process for management. It is a dynamic and complex process – not only because imitators will enter the market, incumbents will also seek to implement a follower type of strategy, or simply because conventional thinking leads decision-makers to adopt a cost leader type of strategy as a response to discount.

Equally important, the introduction of a discount strategy both creates value and generates value destruction. Value is created during the dynamic processes of implementing the discount strategy, illustrated by the continuous price reductions along with constant product or service improvements, which both create value for the diligent discount operator and for its customers. At the same time, immense value destruction is generated for competitors who are unable to respond in a timely fashion and who see market shares disappear and prices erode. Both the incumbent airlines and mobile operators have had this experience.

This raises important new questions for decision-makers in most industries: how much of the value creation and destruction can be foreseen when introducing discount? What are the main issues and procedural steps?

These questions are addressed in this chapter which demonstrates how the notion of discount strategy will become increasingly stimulated in the years to come.

Strategy and war

Clausewitz [1] argued that strategy depends on the basic building blocks which are used in warfare. Thus his perspective on strategy is still relevant – although we don't like the notion of 'war' as such. Throughout the previous chapters it has been illustrated that the execution of a discount strategy both creates value and generates destruction of value at one and the same time.

With regard to value creation, the following examples have been identified:

Like some others, Skype created downloadable software to facilitate free peer-to-peer Voice over IP calls. However, the marketing gimmick was to make the software free of charge, which was unprecedented in the telecommunications industry, creating an exorbitant subscriber in-take and much value for customers, substituting $1 calls per minute with free calls. Although it was easy to imitate Skype, the incumbent players in telecommunications were unable to do so, partly because Skype had already locked in a huge customer base with a zero cost, zero prized product, and partly because of their own revenue loss and subsequent cannibalization.

Ryanair, taking some elements from Southwest Airlines, in a new geographical arena (Northern Europe), revolutionized the airline industry with very low fares paired with a much lower cost-base than that achievable for the incumbents. More cost-efficient planes and flight logistics, high turnover rates, diligent purchase of the plane infrastructure, and user-friendly low-cost front-office and back-office systems meant that Ryanair became and stayed hugely profitable. Ryanair has been imitated but not on their 'own' flight routes where it became impossible for the incumbent flag-carriers to imitate it successfully, partly because Ryanair was the first discount mover on these routes, partly because of the fact that the incumbents were unable to match the cost base of Ryanair. Ryanair actually uses similar a marketing ploy to Skype as Ryan distributes a considerable number of flight tickets for free and communicates the message constantly that Ryanair will take all passengers for free at some stage. All this has generated greater profits to Ryanair and greater value for the customers, but considerable value loss for its incumbent competitors.

Within the mobile phone industry, CBB Mobil changed the cost base of a mobile marketing operation completely. The mobile communications industry has been characterized by prices per minute which are 6–10 times higher than fixed network communication, despite the fact that mobile communication is less costly to produce. However, the mobile incumbents have developed numerous tariff packages, costly and inefficient customer care and billing procedures, plus substantial internal overstaffing. In contrast, CBB Mobil developed a self-care system, no postal bills and only one, much lower, tariff. Again, this created value for the company and the customers, but value destruction for the incumbent operators who now realize that mobile tariffs will decrease dramatically in the future.

Lidl has learned the same lessons: adopting a discount strategy and implementing the business models with 'No Frills' attached. Furthermore, Lidl has differentiated itself with a portfolio of own products, labelled proprietarily, leaving room for a price, quality and retention edge as compared with its competitors. Imitation is possible and numerous discount retail grocery chains have emerged, but no one has so far imitated the idea of having almost completely own discount grocery products labelled proprietarily. In a sense, Lidl attracts double the attention, partly as a discount provider, partly because they are a 'discount' discount provider. This has created profit and customer value, but also value destruction in the markets which Lidl enters. Whenever Lidl enters a market, prices are reported to drop significantly. Although many will argue that the retail discount market is almost saturated it is notable that Lidl, after their entrance on the Danish market in 2005, plans to expand with more than 50 stores in 2006. From a competitor perspective this is seen as an aggressive strategy.

Essentially, discount may be referred to as a kind of warfare in which both value creation and destruction take place. Clausewitz may be remembered especially for having said the following, which has become his working definition of war:

> War is not merely a political act, but also a political instrument, a continuation of political relations, a carrying out of the same by other means.

A common characteristic of Skype, Ryanair, CBB Mobil and Lidl is that they perceive themselves as engaged in warfare. This is reflected in numerous examples such as:

- 'Us' against 'them'.

- 'We are alone on our side of the football pitch fighting against the incumbents on the other side'.

- 'Their weapons are old-fashioned, whereas we come with the new technology'.

- 'They are fat and lazy, we are slim and efficient'.

- 'Their business case deserves to be destroyed'.

- 'We shall conquer in the end'.

- 'We are born to win the price war'.

These attitudes generate benefits for the discount business both internally and externally. Internally, the discount organization benefits from the motivational effects of having a clear vision – the production of better and far cheaper services than the incumbents can deliver. Its employees are prepared to work harder for a lower salary than at the incumbents. Living the discounted brand becomes a part of the organizational behavior.

Referring to Clausewitz, 'war' can be substituted with 'discount' as follows:

> **Discount** is not merely a political act, but also a political instrument, a continuation of political relations, a carrying out of the same by other means.

This is precisely how some of the foremost stakeholders of discount – the customers and the press – perceive the marketing side of discount. Customers and journalists love tensions, conflicts and warfare. The majority of customers are generally more inclined towards David than Goliath, the challenger than the defender, the weaker than the (perceived) stronger. Invariably, this gives the discount strategy a marketing advantage in that it paves the way for free political marketing in the media and lowers or almost extinguishes customer acquisition costs.

The incumbents, on the contrary, typically do not perceive themselves as engaged in warfare. They tend to regard the introduction of discount competitors as a marginal issue, as upstarts who can be ignored, or as *'something which we can deal with at a later stage'*. At some stage – when the discount provider has gained a sustainable foothold on the market – it is typical to see the incumbents either trying to set technical hindrances for the discount competitor (e.g. concerning access to networks, wholesale pricing on an inter-company basis, distribution channels, etc) or begin to complain in public (e.g. the flag-carriers complaining about Ryanair's success with agreements with secondary airports).

Arguably, the incumbents are the natural born loser in this game where discount is ' . . . a political instrument . . . carrying out the same by other means'.

In summary, Figure 12.1 depicts some of the main characteristics of discount warfare.

Means of measurement	Value creation	Value destruction
Completely new cost base	Possibility of affordable and profitable products	'A torpedo hitting the super tanker', since the cost base cannot be changed in the short run
Price war with successive price decrease over time or products priced at zero	Affordable and profitable products, proud employees and loyal customers	Substantial alternative loss in top-line and the withering away of corporate profitability
Customer self-service, auto provision, customer control, the customer as co-producer	Better delivery systems, (perceived) higher service, customer identification with the company and the product	Service delivery becoming old-fashioned overnight, customer churn, employee dissatisfaction
The use of innovative but proven technology	Technology level suits demand	Overinvestment in technology, harming the cost base
Aggressive ('Gorilla-like') marketing	A stronger brand, the value of the brand increases	Cracks begin to appear in the brand, the value of the brand decreases and creates top-line deficit
'No Frills' (product and warfare)	Saving all the peripheral services	More (peripheral) services, i.e. higher cost base

Figure 12.1 Examples of value creation and value destruction in the discount warfare

Strategy revisited

Whereas Lidl appeared to have commenced operations from the outset based on a discount strategy, both Ryanair and CBB undertook a discount strategy as a kind of last resort.

This resembles a story told by Karl Weick, professor at the University of Michigan, about a Hungarian military unit that lost its way in the Alps in a snowstorm [2]:

> Yes, they said, we considered ourselves lost and waited for the end. And one of us found a map in his pocket. That calmed us down. We pitched camp, lasted out the snowstorm, and through the map we discovered our bearings. And here we are. The lieutenant borrowed this remarkable map and had a good look at it. He discovered to his astonishment that it was not a map of the Alps, but a map of the Pyrenees.

The implication of this with regard to the discount strategy is that the 'strategic map' is important in the crafting of the discount organization in order to achieve the desired effectiveness. Alternately, if the 'strategic map' is missing, then it is questionable whether you can demand high performance and diligent output.

This is particularly relevant for Ryanair and CBB Mobil. Both organizations were on the brink of bankruptcy, when they turned around due to the adoption of a discount type strategy. Not all of the elements were present from the outset in order to deploy a non-failure strategy, but the organization got a map, a renewal of its hopes and aspirations, and achieved a new beginning.

However, some years ago, neither Ryanair, nor CBB Mobil had a detailed and 'correct' map to enable the discount development going forward. They adopted the notion of discount and worked from this as a new philosophical background. They did not adopt a mission and vision statement, or introduce expensive branding consultants to support the process. They just did it!

But the interesting question to pose about these few very successful discount organizations is: what does a detailed discount strategy map look like? What do you need to carry in the toolbox? And how is the toolbox to be used in terms of sequences, processes, and other managerial practices?

These questions will be addressed in the context of execution.

The building blocks of the discount strategy model

The execution of a discount strategy may take various forms, but the starting point is to map strategically what discount is really about. The building blocks of the discount strategy model as well as the more detailed content of the framework have been mapped in Figure 12.2. The discount strategy model was described generically in Chapter 7, including the introduction of the four building blocks. The discount model has been further developed in order to cater for the specific findings on the discount product (Chapter 8), branding (Chapter 9), the customers (Chapter 10) and the technology issues (Chapter 11).

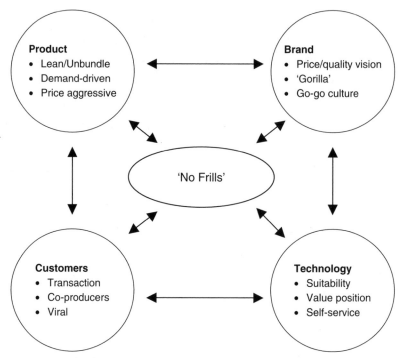

Figure 12.2 The detailed discount strategy model – the four building blocks of the crafting of a discount strategy

The successful execution of a discount strategy requires a number of factors in an equation which is dynamic. Figure 12.2 represents the common denominator of the discount business cases analysed more in detail in Chapters 4, 5 and 6. Although the model does not pretend to be fully comprehensive and exhaustive it illustrates the most important criteria for how to obtain success.

The discount product is the pivotal point for the discount philosophy. The starting point is to craft a product which is lean and unbundled, leaving room for transparency, self-service, and providing a contrast to the ever increasing number of peripheral services attached to conventional products. However, low price and subsequent price decreases are key to the crafting of the discount product. If there is no room for aggressive pricing on a continuous basis, the product will simply lose its status as a discount product. The aggressive price has a knock-on effect on the demand-driven nature of the discount product owing to the rapidly increasing substitution effects. These effects are increased the more the discount product is aligned with the customers' needs.

In the discussion of a *good brand*, some of the main findings were that the discount vision of low prices along with high quality is a good starting point in the branding process. There is no major need for huge out of pocket spending in the establishment of a discount brand and it does not make sense as in conventional strategy to invest in Corporate Social Responsibility programs in order to justify the company. With the price/quality vision, the company is justified per se. The inexpensive branding is also due to the political marketing of the company, the 'Mr Company'-effect, the Gorilla image, and the in-company 'discount' culture.

The addressable customer is also an important factor in the discount strategy, because the customer is the social capital of the company. Translated into marketing, this implies that conventional relationship marketing – where customer segments are treated differently – is to be replaced by a pure transaction-based formula, whereby the customers are treated equally. Egalitarian status, when consuming a discount product, is the basis of the WOM-effect, which, in turn, develops the customers into active viral ambassadors for the product. This is further underlined by the fact that the customers are allowed to function as co-producers, thereby breaking down the traditional wall between production and consumption of a product.

Adequate technology is the last element in the building of the discount strategy. First of all, the chosen technology needs to be suitable. This may often be translated into a 'play safe' position where the discount operation opts for proven technology instead of the conventional 'overinvestment' in new or rather the newest technology. Furthermore, scalability is an issue to be addressed. Another salient issue is to co-think the technology with the value chain considerations of the discount strategy.

Having crafted the discount strategy 'building' based on these four building blocks, attention should also be paid to the glue of the building which at all times is the 'No Frills' concept. 'No Frills' are important for a number of reasons:

- The discount product is by definition a 'No Frills' product. The entire product development is preconditioned on the farewell to frills.

- It is far easier to build a brand based on 'No Frills' than to deal with a high degree of complexity which often generates dilution of a brand.

- The target customers do not like frills and the discretionary award of extra peripheral services delivered to other customers. Rather, 'No Frills' supports the social aspiration to treat every customer equally according to the egalitarian principle.

- In many organizations the decision making process often favours fancy new technology, maybe unproven, and most certainly based on elements of frills. The suitable technology for discount is technology with 'No Frills'.

However, 'No Frills' as the glue appears when we look at the dynamic nature of the discount model outlined in Figure 12.2. A brand with 'No Frills' attached interacts perfectly well with customers, who are attracted by 'No Frills', and therefore, in turn, contribute to the strengthening of the 'No Frills' element in the brand formula. Another example of 'No Frills' as the glue is the dynamic relationship between the product and the technology. A lean, unbundled product based on 'No Frills' makes it easier to design suitable technology for the discount business as the technology is simpler and easier to develop when the frills do not have to be taken into account. Conversely, proven, scalable and simple technology makes it easier to conduct the product development in sync with the corporate discount strategy.

The dynamic nature of the execution of discount has been touched upon several times. In the last section, some of the dynamism in the discount strategy development and execution processes will be touched upon briefly.

The various execution processes

As stated, execution is an important driver in getting discount strategies (as well as other strategies) to work (see the $4 + 2$ model in *What Really Works*).

Much attention is normally focused upon organization hurdles, motivational effects, the issue of trust, etc when engaged in strategy development. Just imagine how difficult it is in conventional strategy and organizational process to switch from a differentiator type of strategy to the cost leader type of strategy. Numerous redundancies, lay-offs, cost cutting exercises, and profit improvement programs generate fear, instability and conflicts in and around the traditional organization.

However, in the case of discount strategy, everything seems to be simpler. In terms of processes this is either because most discount companies start from scratch, whereby the execution processes have no existing hurdles to take into account (cf. the cases of Skype and Lidl), or because organizations changing from another strategy into discount come from the state of a crisis and are fighting to survive (cf. the cases of Skype, Ryanair, and CBB Mobil).

Regarding the generic content of a strategy, which was outlined as either differentiation or cost leadership in the traditional strategy thinking, this distinction is abolished in a discount strategy. As such this strategy takes on a much more integrated perspective.

A discount strategy allows for differentiation and cost leadership at one and the same time. Consequently, it proved relatively easy to further develop, e.g. Ryanair and CBB Mobil into discount operations.

Some of the main elements and issues of the execution processes are now to be extracted. The starting point is Figure 12.3 where a phased approach is outlined.

Following this model, caution is taken into account. Rather than start up quickly and run into problems at an early stage, the prudent discount strategist has the patience to develop the winning formula right from the beginning. The litmus test is the customer, as recognized during phases 1 and 2 of Figure 12.3. When they are supporting the discount business idea and the implementation hereof enthusiastically, it is time to move.

Once the discount business case is up and running successfully, the environment will become shocked and will display a variety of strange and, from time to time, irrational reactions, as indicated in phase 3. The skilled executer can rest assured that most – if not all – of such reactions can be turned to advantages by the discount business.

The execution of a the discount business model – an example

Phase 1:   Framing the creative work

Make up your business plan based on your preferred template and number crunching techniques and include thorough analysis and creative development around the four cornerstones.

Phase 2:   Setting the stage behind the stage

Initially, test whether your first customer sample likes the product and will become viral ambassadors. After this pilot trial you fine tune your marketing strategy and plan for the achievement of the Gorilla effect. In order to rely on the first mover and/or surprise effect, all these preparations are behind the stage.

Phase 3:   Taking the environment by surprise

Go live! Hope for overreactions from competitors (as this will give you extra media coverage). Get the media onboard in order to obtain free-of-charge promotion, e.g. by way of 'Mr. Company'.

Phase 4:   Galvanizing the business case

Use the dynamism of the discount model in Figure 12.2 and continuously work with the four building blocks and the 'No Frills' glue. You have started a perpetual wheel with many reinforcing factors if you manage to take up 3–4% of the market during the first 12 months.

Figure 12.3   The phased approach to the execution process

Not only lazy incumbents, cosy duopolies, born monopolists, and state-aided companies, but also all competitors will be met by tough challenges overnight and even well-off companies may find it more difficult to survive than ever. Discount strategies executed successfully imply value creation and value destruction at one and the same time! How to maintain the business is the bottom line in phase 4.

13

Epilogue

How to reflect thoroughly on the wider repercussions of successful discount business strategies?

Having described the initial faltering of the oxymoron of existing strategies and the revolutionary nature of discount business strategies, it is now time to turn to reflections relevant to both 'camps'.

One camp is characterized by the entrepreneurs who would like to break through the wall with a discount business strategy. Having familiarized oneself with the discount business model and the focus on execution in this book, the entrepreneur asks eagerly: what are the key questions I now have to address?

The other camp is characterized by managers in incumbent companies, probably with a good track record, high market share, and a decent level of company profitability and above average personal remuneration packages. In most cases, they would not have read this book, and even if, somewhat involuntarily, they did read it, their approach to wider reflections would be difficult. Some would probably not ask questions at all and just acquiesce in the approach that 'discount will never be a rose that can grow in our garden'. A few will probably become shell-shocked and ask immediately: 'What are the key questions to address with regard to the potential dangers ahead?'

Invariably, the business strategy researcher may take a more neutral stand and keep an eye on the theoretical implications and implications related to the trajectories between theory and real life.

Taken all together, the eager entrepreneur, the incumbent manager and the business strategy researcher constitute the most important background to an understanding of the future successes and failures of discount business strategies. Consequently, all three angles are shown in Figure 13.1.

The 10 most salient issues	The eager entrepreneur	The incumbent manager	The business strategy researcher
1. Mission – viz. what is the role and rationale of the discount operation?	How can I achieve a situational 'monopoly' as the first mover?	Isn't it the wisest thing to wait and see whether discount gains foothold?	The successful first mover will always have a strategic advantage
2. Vision – viz. how ambitious is the discounter?	What am I to do if I wish to be the market leader and quickly gain a 50% market share?	Can't we rest assured according to Porter that a mixed discount strategy will always fail?	In selected industries there will always be room for a 25–75% discount market share
3. Product – viz. what should the product look like?	How is it possible to focus on and even improve the core product at a lower price?	Haven't our market researchers found out that our customers prefer peripheral services regardless?	The conventional trade off between quality and price no longer always prevails

Figure 13.1 Key questions to address concerning the crafting and execution of the discount business strategy

4. Brand – viz. how much does it take to build and retain a brand?	Which steps do I take in order to achieve branding effects at no cost? Where is the Gorilla in this industry?	How much do we need to increase our marketing budget in order to fight discount operations?	Political mass marketing and corporate social responsibility issues are decoupled from marketing spending
5. Customers – viz. what is the role of the customer?	How do my tactics look like in order to make customers co-produce my products?	Why shouldn't our customers continue to be consumers only?	The traditional borderline between consumption and production is becoming increasingly unclear
6. Technology – viz. which one is the most optimal technology platform of the company?	How do I find a proven technology with a good track record and scalability?	How do we continue to be at the cutting edge of the newest technology?	Disruptive technology is seldom the most advanced technology
7. Management – viz. which key qualifications should the top management possess?	Where do I find top management who has the aggressiveness to fight against incumbents?	Hasn't it proved a prudent strategy to recruit top level management with experience from large organizations?	Recruitment of management is key to values and mental programming of organizations
8. Staff – viz. what is the approach to remuneration and qualifications?	How do I make below average remuneration and above average performance requirements work?	Experience will continue to be decisive. Why should we leave our principle making staff earn more the longer they stay?	Many staff members are much more attracted to the culture and values than remuneration in itself
9. Stakeholders – viz. who are the main stakeholders to serve?	How do we serve customers, opinion leaders, chat groups, consumer boards etc? How do I invent and integrate new stakeholders?	How do we continue to serve our stakeholders?	The concept of stakeholders continue to be broader and broader
10. The business plan development – viz. what is the core competence in the development of the business strategy	How do we invent, rethink, cut to the core, free ride, exploit creativity, develop a new level playing field, show up as the industry Gorilla, etc.?	Why shouldn't the possibility of discounters entering 'our' market be dealt with in our experience strategic planning program?	Strategy is no longer a fully rational process, and strategies as well as industry logics change dynamically, due to e.g. creativity and unforeseen events

Figure 13.1 Continued

The discount kaleidoscope tells us that huge value creation and potentially excessive value destruction are part of the rapid, unpredictable change in numerous industries. The eager entrepreneur has good prospects of pursuing a discount business strategy, addressing the key questions of Figure 13.1, as was the case with the entrepreneurs behind Ryanair, Lidl and CBB Mobil.

However, the incumbent manager will address the same type of questions, however widely different and, mostly, will try to sweep discount under the existing corporate carpet. This may be a wise strategy because the incumbent is often deadlocked. It has proved difficult for incumbents to establish and add on discount products to their existing portfolio without changing the organization. This was the case with Swissair, Sabena, SAS and many others within the airline industry. In the mobile communications business this has, so far, also been the case with all incumbents as is also the case with many incumbent grocery retailers. Interestingly, incumbents have also failed to pursue discount strategies successfully in unbundled organizations, e.g. the former Go of British Airways and Easy Mobile of TDC.

As these appear to be the main trends, some of the new winners of tomorrow will be born out of the road map of a discount business strategy. This is partly because a prudent discount road map is a self-contained success, and partly because the DNA-structure of the incumbents is based on the oxymoron between a differentiation and cost leader strategy. Most incumbents do not see the perils ahead!

In business strategy research, however, we expect to see more focus on the discount business strategy framework in the future and the withering away of the oxymoron between differentiation and cost leadership. The relationship between strategy theory and business practice will soon reach a new equilibrium!

In practice, we expect more companies to break out from the traditional way of strategic thinking. In the future we expect more companies to pursue discount strategies. The challenge for most companies will be to develop new strategies for accelerating the time it takes to deliver new business solutions to their customers. Many companies will be busy developing new strategies.

Notes

1. Why are some companies more successful than others?

[1] Peters, T.J. & Waterman, R.H. (1982) *Search of Excellence.* Harper & Row.
[2] Deal, T.E. & Kennedy, A.A. (1982) *Corporate Culture.* Addison Wesley.
[3] Collins, J.C. & Porras, J.I. *Build to Last.* Harper Collins. 1994.
[4] Collins, J.C. (2001) *Good to Great, Why Some Companies Make the Leap... and Others Don't.* New York: BookHouse Publishing.
[5] Joyce, W. & Nohria. N. (2003) *What Really Works: The* $4 + 2$ *Formula for Sustained Business Success.* Collins.
[6] Kim, W.C. & Mauborgne, R. (2005) *Blue Ocean Strategy. How to Create Uncontested Market Space and Make the Competition Irrelevant.* Harvard Business School Press.
[7] Schumpeter, J.A. (1942) *Capitalism, Socialism, and Democracy.* New York: Harper.
[8] http://www.woopidoo.com/business_quotes/business-quotes.htm.
[9] Ingvar Kamprad and IKEA, Harvard Business School.
[10] Costco – The Leader's Challenges, ICFAI Business School, 2003.
[11] Ibid.
[12] FCC, Annual International Teleco Communications Data, 2003 (latest available).

2. The oxymoron of existing strategies: where do we go from here?

[1] Porter, M. (1985) *Competitive Advantage: Creating and Sustaining Superior Performance.* Free Press, p. 12.
[2] Ibid.

[3] Hambrick, D. (1983) An Emperical Typology of Mature Industrial-Product Environment. *Academy of Management Journal*, pp. 467–488.

[4] Dess, G. & Davis, P. (1984) Porter's (1980) Generic Strategies as Determinants of Strategy Group Membership and Organizational Performance. *Academy of Management Journal*, 27(3), p. 467.

[5] O'Farrel, P.N., Hitchens, D.M. & Moffat, L.A.R. (1993) The Competitive Advantage of Business Service Firms: A Matched Pairs Analysis of the Relationship between Generic Strategy and Performance. *The Service Industries Journal*, 13(1), pp. 40–64.

[6] Mintzberg, H., Ahlstrand, B. & Lampel, J. (1998) *Strategy Safari. The Complete Guide Through the Wilds of Strategic Management.* Prentice Hall, pp. 118–120.

[7] Miller, D. & Friesen, P. (1996A) Porter's (1980) Generic Strategies and Performance: An Empirical Examination with American Data. Part II. Performance Implications. *Organizational Studies.* 7(1), pp. 255–261.

[8] Miller, D. & Friesen, P. (1996B) Porter's (1980) Generic Strategies and Performance: An Empirical Examination with American Data. Part I. Testing Porter. *Organizational Studies*, 7(3), pp. 37–55.

[9] Mintzberg, H., Ahlstrand, B. & Lampel, J. (1998) *Strategy Safari. The Complete Guide Through the Wilds of Strategic Management.* Prentice Hall, p. 120.

[10] Murray, A. (1998) A Contingency View of Porter's Generic Strategies. *Academy of Management Journals Review*, 13(3), pp. 390–400.

[11] Gilbert, X. & Strebel, P. (1987) Strategies to Outplace the Competition. *Journal of Business Strategy*, p. 28.

[12] Miller, D. (1993) The Generic Trap. *Journal of Business Strategy*, pp. 37–41.

[13] Normann, R. (2000) *Service Management. Strategy and Leadership in Service Business.* 3rd edn. John Wiley & Sons Ltd.

[14] Normann, R. (2000) *Service Management. Strategy and Leadership in Service Business.* 3rd edn. John Wiley & Sons Ltd. pp. 75–82.

[15] Kotler, A. & Armstrong, G. (2004) *Principles of Marketing.* 10th edn. Prentice Hall.

[16] Normann, R. (2000) *Service Management. Strategy and Leadership in Service Business.* 3rd edn. John Wiley & Sons Ltd. p. 77.

[17] Normann, R. (2000) *Service Management. Strategy and Leadership in Service Business.* 3rd edn. John Wiley & Sons Ltd. p. 21.

[18] Kim, W.C. & Mauborgne, R. (2005) *Blue Ocean Strategy. How to Create Uncontested Market Space and Make the Competition Irrelevant.* Harvard Business School Press, p. 13.

[19] Kim, W.C. & Mauborgne, R. (2005) *Blue Ocean Strategy. How to Create Uncontested Market Space and Make the Competition Irrelevant.* Harvard Business School Press, p. 126.

4. CBB

[1] The authors were one of the former owners of the shares of CBB and active at the Board level, respectively. All the information in the case description derives from information within the public domain.

[2] With regard to mobile communications, Denmark is an interesting geographical starting point, as not only were the radio waves for commercial use invented by a Danish engineer (Valdemar Poulsen) but also because of early adoption and penetration as compared with many other countries.

[3] Cf., e.g. the debates on www.mobildebat.dk.

[4] Based on an analysis from the Consumer Information Board.

[5] Cf., e.g. the analysis in Berlingske Tidendes Nyhedsmagasin, No. 26, 15–21 September 2003, pp. 26–29. In this context it should also be noted that the analysis lists an overview of the risks attached to the CBB business case. These risks are not described in the case story and for good reason since the risks never materialized.

[6] Strand Consult. (2004). *The Moment of Truth*. Copenhagen.

[7] The transaction took place on 30 April 2004 when Sonofon, on whose network CBB makes service provision, bought 100 % of the shares in CBB Mobil A/S.

[8] Studies by investment Bank Gudme Raaschou in connection with an analysis by the National Telecom Agency on competition.

[9] Investment Bank 'Danske Equities' has made a financial analysis of TDC's average charge out per minute and has arrived at a figure equal to DKK 2.30 including VAT and DKK 1.84 excluding VAT (€ 0.25). This compares to DKK 0.69 (€ 0.09) including VAT and DKK 0.55 (€ 0.07) excluding VAT at CBB.

5. Lidl

[1] Retail Institute Scandinavia A/S, *Supermarket of the future*, Conference 17 January 2005. p. 5.

[2] M+M Planet Retail, Top 30 Grocery Retailers Worldwide, 2004.

[3] Retail Institute Scandinavia, *When the discount store is sufficient, the supermarket and the brands will die.*

[4] Retail Institute Scandinavia A/S, *Supermarket of the future*, Conference 17 January 2005, p. 5.

[5] This section draws upon Jan Furstenborg. *The Schwarz Group (Lidl)*, 1 March 2004, UNI Commerce.

[6] Interview with Bruno Christensen, 20 January 2005.

[7] AC Nielsen, *What can we expect from Lidl?* Presentation from 8 April 2003.

[8] McKinsey Quarterly, 2004 Number 4: *Europeans warm to bargain groceries*.

[9] Figure based on Exhibit 2 from the article *Europe warms to bargain groceries*, McKinsey Quarterly.

[10] Retail Institute Scandinavia, *When the discount store is sufficient, the supermarket and the brands will die.*

[11] Survey conducted by Retail Institute Scandinavia among Danish customers.

[12] *Brand versus Private Labels*, John Stanley.

[13] Interview with Retail Institute Scandinavia, 20 January 2005.

[14] AC Nielsen, *What can we expect from Lidl?* Presentation of 8 April 2003.

[15] Carin Petterson criticizes massive Lidl coverge. http://pub.tv2.no/nettavisen/english/article270608.ece

[16] Retail Institute Scandinavia, *When the discount store is sufficient, the supermarket and the brands will die.*

[17] AC Nielsen, *What can we expect from Lidl?* Presentation of 8 April 2003.

[18] M+M Planet Retail, Top 30 Grocery Retailers, 2003. www. planetretail.net.

6. Ryanair

[1] AirlinesGate – http://airlinesgate.free.fr/articles/industry4.htm.

[2] Rivkin, J.W. (2000). *Dogfight over Europe*, Harvard Business Case.

[3] Rivkin, J.W. (2000). *Dogfight over Europe*, Harvard Business Case.

[4] http://irish.typepad.com/irisheyes/2004/week22/.

[5] Ryanair Annual Report – Financial presentation 2003 & data from IATA.

[6] Rivkin, J.W. (2000). *Dogfight over Europe*, Harvard Business Case.

[7] Rivkin, J.W. (2000). *Dogfight over Europe*, Harvard Business Case.

[8] Ryanair Annual Report 2001.

[9] Annual Reports for easyJet, Virgin Express, BA and Aer Lingus.

[10] Interview with Michael O'Leary conducted by Sebastian Steinke in 2004, Motor-Presse Stuttgart.

[11] Ryanair Annual Report 2002.

[12] Ryanair Financial Roadshow 2003. It should be noted that the figures are produced by Ryanair themselves. However, they do not seem to have been disputed.
[13] Skytrax research – http://www.airlinequality.com/Forum/ryan.htm.
[14] AFX Europe (Focus); February 2004.
[15] Eurocontrol 2003.

8.   The attractiveness of the core product

[1] Kennedy, R.F. (1969) *Thirteen Days*. Pan Books p. 72. In fact, we feel that the business manager is better off searching for ways to avoid loss of control and subsequent disruption in the literature of political science, sociology, psychology, etc (on 'crisis'). The business manager will be unable to find the appropriate answers in today's management and strategy literature.
[2] It should be noted that Ryanair fares are not included in AEA's estimates.
[3] Strand Consult. (2004) *The Moment of Truth*. Copenhagen.
[4] Kotler, P. & Keller, K.L. (2004) *Marketing Management*. 12th edn, Prentice Hall.
[5] Kotler, P. & Armstrong, G. (2004) *Principles of Marketing*. 10th edn, Prentice Hall.
[6] Source for graph: ACI annual conference 2005 – presentation.

9.   A good brand is much more than a good brand

[1] Aaker, D.A. & Joachimsthaler, E. (2002) *Brand Leadership*. Simon & Schuster, UK Ltd. Cf. in particular the description at p. 68 of the so-called *'different-paradigm brands'* under which category successful discount brands also operate, although discount brands are not addressed directly.

[2] Hatch, M.J. & Schultz, M. (2001) Are the Strategic Stars Aligned for Your Corporate Brand? *Harvard Business Review*, pp. 129–134. which addresses this gap specifically.

[3] Cf. note (i), in particular at pp. 264–266. Again discount brands are not addressed specifically.

[4] Mintzberg, H., Ahlstrand, B. & Lampel, J. (1998) *Strategy Safari. The Complete Guide through the Wilds of Strategic Management.* Prentice Hall.

[5] Cf. note (i), p. 131.

[6] Harrisson, R. (2003) Corporate Social Responsibility and the Consumer Movement. *Consumer Policy Review* 13(4), p. 127.

[7] We therefore disagree with Milton Friedman, *The Social Responsibility of Business Is to Increase Profit*, New York Times Magazine, September 1970 and also in Hofmann, W.M., Frederick, R.E. & Schwartz, M.S (2001) *Business Ethics – Reading and Cases in Corporate Morality*, Mc Graw-Hill, pp. 156–160. The modern firm in the affluent society has a social responsibility and often a need for justification of social responsibility. However, the discount company is generally justified per se.

10. The discount customer and social capital

[1] Putnam, R. (1993) *Making Democracy Work. Civic traditions in modern Italy*. Princeton University Press.

[2] Cf. Coleman, J.S. (1988) Social Capital in the Creation of Human Capital. *American Journal of Sociology*, pp. 94–120.

[3] Mossberg, L. (2003) *Att skapa upplevelser – fram OK til WOW*. Studentliteratur, Lund. Notwithstanding the fact that Lena Mossberg describes primarily event driven cases like entertainment, cultural institutions and sports clubs, we think that her description of the WOW-effect leads directly forward to the WOM-effect which has a general applicability far beyond her own descriptions.

[4] Uslaner, E.M. (2001) *The Moral Foundations of Trust*. Cambridge University Press, and *Trust and Corruption*, paper to University of Salford conference.

[5] Cf., e.g. Kotler, P., Armstrong, G., Saunders, J., & Wong, V. (1999) *Principles of Marketing*. Princeton Hall, Cf. also Hougaard, S. & Bjerre, M. (2002) *Strategic Relationship Marketing*. Samfundslitteratur. In particular Figure 1–11 at p. 46 presents a good overview of main relationship marketing approaches. When we address the relationship marketing

approach it is based on what is called '*The Marketing Management*' where segmentation and customer loyalty is key.

[6] Hougaard, S. & Bjerre, M. (2002) *Strategic Relationship Marketing.* Samfundslitteratur, p. 322: *Flight Bonus: The Most Successful Loyalty Program Ever.*

[7] Festinger, L. (1957) *Theory of cognitive dissonance.* Stanford University Press.

[8] Sharp, B. & Dawes, J. (2001) What is Differentiation and How Does It Work? *Journal of Marketing Management*, 17, pp. 739–759.

11. Finding the suitable technology

[1] Peter, T.J. & Waterman, R.H. (1982) *In Search of Excellence. Lessons from America's Best-Run Companies.* Harper & Row, New York. In particular, the description at p. 195 is of interest it: Peters and Waterman appraise Digital because of its focus on serving the sophisticated technology needs of the customer, while later this appeared to be an overshooting of technology with grave effects for Digital: 'It's surprising how little they've caused their own growth. For years, they've been dragged along by interesting applications their customers came up with'.

[2] Collins, J. (2001) *Good to Great, Why Some Companies Make the Leap . . . and Others Don't.* BookHouse Publishing.

[3] Nohria, N., Joyce, W. & Roberson, B. (2003) What Really Works. *Harvard Business Review.* July

[4] Christensen, C.M. & Raynor, M.E. (2003) *The Innovative Solution. Creating and Sustaining Successful Growth.* Harvard Business School Press. p. 33.

[5] Ibid, p. 34. It is remarkable that there seems to be a lot of confusion regarding the term 'disruption', cf. ibid p. 66: 'Hence, many people have equated our use of the term 'sustaining' innovation with their preexisting from of 'incremental' innovation, and they have equated the term disruptive technology with the words radical, breakthrough, out-of-the-box, or different. They then conclude that disruptive ideas (as they define them) are good and merit investment. We regret that this happens, because our findings relate to at very specific definition of disruptiveness, as stated in our text here. It is for this reason that in this book we have substituted the term disruptive technology – to minimize the chance that readers will twist the concept to fit into what we believe is an incorrect way of categorizing the circumstances'.

12. Value creation and value destruction

[1] Clausewitz, C. von (1989) *On War*. Princeton University Press.
[2] Weick, K.E. (1995) *Sensemaking in Organizations*. Sage Publications, p. 54.

Bibliography

Abell, D.F. (1993) *Managing with Dual Strategies. Mastering the Present. Preempting the Future.* Free Press.

Andrews, K.R. (1971) *The Concept of Corporate Strategy.* Homewood, IL. Irwin.

Ansoff, H.I. (1965) *Corporate Strategy.* Penguin Modern Management Readings.

Argyris, C. & Schön, D.A. (1974) *Theory in Practice: Increasing Professional Effectiveness.* San Francisco. Jossey-Bass.

Barney, J.B. & Hesterly, W.S. (2006) *Strategic Management and Competitive Advantage. Concepts and Cases.* Pearson-Prentice Hall.

Chandler, A. (1962) *Strategy and Structure: Chapters in the History of the Industrial Enterprise.* Cambridge. The MIT Press.

Clausewitz, Carl Von. (1997) *On War.* Wordsworth Editions.

Chakravarthy, B., Mueller-Stewens, B. & Lorange, P. (2002) *Strategy Process: Shaping the Contours of the Field.* Blackwell Publishing.

Christensen, C.M. & Raynor, M.E. (2003) *The Innovative Solution. Creating and Sustaining Successful Growth.* Harvard Business School Press.

Christensen, C.M., Johnson, M.W. & Rigby, D.K. (2002) Foundations for Growth: How To Identify and Build Disruptive New Businesses. *MIT Sloan Management Review.* 43(3), pp. 22–31.

Collins, J.C. & Porras, J.I. (1994) *Build to Last.* Harper Collins.

Collins, J. (2001) *Good to Great. Why Some Companies Make the Leap . . . and Others Don't.* BookHouse Publishing.

Coulter, M. (2005) *Strategic Management in Action.* (3rd edn) Pearson Educational International.

Day, G.S. & Reibstein, D.J. (1997) *Wharton on Dynamic Competitive Strategy.* John Wiley & Sons Ltd.

De Wit, B. & Meyer, R. (2005) *Strategy Synthesis. Resolving Strategy Paradoxes to Create Competitive Advantages.* (2nd edn) Thomson.

Deal, T.E. & Kennedy, A.A. (1982) *Corporate Culture.* Addison Wesley.

Deans, G.K. & Kroeger, F. (2004) *Stretch How Great Companies Grow in Good Times and Bad*. John Wiley & Sons Ltd.

D'Aveni, R.D. (1994) *Hypercompetition: Managing the Dynamics of Strategic Maneuvering*. Free Press.

Eisenhardt, K.M. & Brown (1998) *Competing on the Edge*. Harvard Business School Press.

Eisenhardt, K.M. & Sull, D.N. (2001) Strategy as Simple Rules *Harvard Business Review*, pp. 107–116.

Grant, R.M. (1991) The Resource-Based Theory of Competitive Advantage: Implications for Strategy Formulation. *California Management Review*, pp. 114–129.

Haberberg, A. & Rieple, A. (2001) *The Strategic Management of Organisations*. Financial Times/Prentice Hall. Harlow.

Hamel, G. & Prahalad, C.K. (1994) *Competing for the Future*. Harvard Business School Press.

Hamel, G. (2000) *Leading the Revolution*. Harvard Business School Press.

Hamel, G. (1996) Strategy as Revolution *Harvard Business Review*. July–August, pp. 69–82.

Hamel, G. & Heene, A. (1994) *Competence-based competition*. John Wiley & Sons Ltd.

Henderson, B. (1979) *Henderson on Corporate Strategy* ABT Books.

Joyce, W. & Nohria, N. (2003) *What Really Works: The 4+2 Formula for Sustained Business Success*.

Johnson, G., Scholes, K. & Whittington, R. (2005) *Exploring Corporate Strategy. Text and Cases*. (7th edn) Prentice Hall.

Kaplan, R.S. & Norton, D.P. (1996) *The Balanced Scorecard: Translating strategy into action*. Harvard Business School Press.

Kim, W.C. & Mauborgne, R. (2005) *Blue Ocean Strategy. How to Create Uncontested Market Space and Make the Competition Irrelevant*. Harvard Business School Press.

Kotler, P. & Armstrong, G. (2004) *Principles of Marketing* (10th edn) Prentice Hall.

Kotler, P. & Keller, K.L. (2004) *Marketing Management* (12th edn) Prentice Hall.

Lele, M.M. (1992) *Creating Strategic Leverage. Matching Company Strengths with Market Opportunities*. John Wiley & Sons Ltd.

Lorange, P. (1980) *Corporate Planning: An Executive Viewpoint*. Prentice Hall.

Lorange, P., Chakravarthy, B., Roos, J. & Van de Ven, A. (1993) *Implementing Strategic Processes. Change, Learning & Co-operation*. Blackwell Business.

Lynch, R. (2006) *Corporate Strategy* (4th edn) FT Prentice Hall.

Mazzucato, M. (ed.) (2002) *Strategy for Business*. Sage Publication.

McKiernan, P. (ed.) (1996) *Historical Evolution of Strategic Management.* Vol.I & II. Aldershot. Dartmouth.

Miles, R.E. & Snow, C.C. (1995) *Fit, Failure & the Hall of Fame.* Free Press.

Mintzberg, H. (1994) *The Rise and Fall of Strategic Planning.* Prentice Hall.

Mintzberg, H., Ahlstrand, B. & Lampel, J. (1998) *Strategy Safari. The Complete Guide Through the Wilds of Strategic Management.* Prentice Hall.

Moore, J.F. (1996) *The Death of Competition. Leadership & Strategy in the Age of Business Ecosystems.* HarperBusiness.

Nadler, D.A. & Slywotsky. A.J. (2004) Strategy and Organization Consulting. In Greiner, L. & Poulfelt, F. (eds), *Handbook of Management Consulting – The Contemporary Consultant.* Thomson: South-Western.

Nonaka, I. & Takeuchi, H. (1995) *The Knowledge-Creating Company: How Japanese Companies Create the Dynamics of Innovation.* Oxford University Press.

Normann, R. (2000) *Service Management. Strategy and Leadership in Service Business* (3rd edn) John Wiley & Sons Ltd.

Ohmae, K. (1985) *Triad Power: The Coming of Global Competition.* McMillan.

Peters, T.J. & Waterman, R.H. (1982) *Search of Excellence.* Harper & Row.

Porter, M.E. (1980) *Competitive Advantage: Creating and Sustaining Superior Performance.* Free Press.

Porter, M.E. (1985) *Competitive Advantage: Creating and Sustaining Superior Performance.* Free Press.

Porter, M.E. (1996) What is Strategy? *Harvard Business Review.* November–December, pp. 61–78.

Prahalad, C.K. & Hamel, G. (1990) The Core Competence of the Corporation. *Harvard Business Review.* May–June, pp. 79–93.

Quinn, J.B., Mintzberg, H. & James, R. (1988) *The Strategy Process.* Prentice Hall.

Shank, J.K. & Govindarajan, V. (1993) *Strategic Cost Management. The New Tool for Competitive Advantage.* Free Press.

Thompson, J.D. (1967) *Organizations in action.* McGraw-Hill.

Tzu, S. (1963) *The Art of War.* Oxford University Press.

Volberda, H.W. & Elfring, T. (2001) *Rethinking Strategy.* Sage Publications.

Whittington, R. (2001) *What is strategy–and does it matter!* (2nd edn) Thomson Learning.

Index